A New Star-Rating System & Other Exciting News from Frommer's!

In our continuing effort to publish the savviest, most up-to-date, and most appealing travel guides available, we've added some great new features.

Frommer's guides now include a new **star-rating system.** Every hotel, restaurant, and attraction is rated from 0 to 3 stars to help you set priorities and organize your time.

We've also added **seven brand-new features** that point you to the great deals, in-the-know advice, and unique experiences that separate travelers from tourists. Throughout the guide, look for:

Finds	Special finds—those places only insiders know about
Fun Fact	Fun facts—details that make travelers more informed and their trips more fun
Kids	Best bets for kids—advice for the whole family
Moments	Special moments—those experiences that memories are made of
Overrated	Places or experiences not worth your time or money
Tips	Insider tips—some great ways to save time and money
Value	Great values—where to get the best deals

Here's what critics say about Frommer's:

"Amazingly easy to use. Very portable, very complete."

—*Booklist*

"Detailed, accurate, and easy-to-read information for all price ranges."

—*Glamour Magazine*

"Hotel information is close to encyclopedic."

—*Des Moines Sunday Register*

"Frommer's Guides have a way of giving you a real feel for a place."

—*Knight Ridder Newspapers*

Frommer's®

PORTABLE
Phoenix & Scottsdale

2nd Edition

by Karl Samson

with Jane Aukshunas

WILEY

Wiley Publishing, Inc.

Published by:

WILEY PUBLISHING, INC.
909 Third Ave.
New York, NY 10022

ISBN 0-7645-6735-7
ISSN 1532-9895

Editor: Liz Albertson
Production Editor: Suzanna R. Thompson
Photo Editor: Richard Fox
Cartographer: John Decamillis
Production by Wiley Indianapolis Composition Services

For information on our other products and services or to obtain technical support, please contact our Customer Care Department within the U.S. at 800-762-2974, outside the U.S. at 317-572-3993 or fax 317-572-4002.

Wiley also publishes its books in a variety of electronic formats. Some content that appears in print may not be available in electronic formats.

Manufactured in the United States of America

5 4 3 2 1

Contents

in Biking in South Mountain or Papago Park. The
these two desert parks are ideal for mountain biking,
her you're a novice making your first foray onto the
udding downhill racer, you'll find miles of riding that
ur speed. See p. 111.

the Day at a Spa. When it comes to stress relief,
ing like a massage or an herbal wrap. The chance to
d do nothing at all is something few of us take the
ymore. For the price of a single 1-hour treatment,
ally spend the whole day using the spa's facilities
, sauna, and all). See p. 123.

the Boyce Thompson Arboretum (east of
is botanical garden is filled with desert plantings
he world—a fascinating place for an educational
sert. See p. 146.

Apache Trail (east of Phoenix): Much of this
ollows a rugged route once ridden by Apaches.
f the most remote country you'll find in the
th far-reaching desert vistas and lots to see and
. See "The Apache Trail," in chapter 9.

ff Dwellings at Tonto National Monument
Located east of Phoenix on the Apache Trail,
nly easily accessible cliff dwellings in Arizona
xplore up close. See p. 146.

Casa Grande Ruins National Monument
Unlike most of the other ruins in the state,
ual structure is built of packed desert soil.
lexing. See p. 148.

urses

Course (Carefree, near Phoenix; © 800/
ever seen a photo of someone teeing off
cing rock and longed to play that same
about playing the Boulders South
desert-style design plays around and
nassive boulders for which the resort is

Wigwam Golf and Country Club
oenix; © 623/935-3811): If you're a
s those cactus- and rattlesnake-filled

List of Maps

ABOUT THE AUTHORS

Karl Samson and **Jane Aukshunas,** husband-and-wife travel-writing team, find that the sunny winter skies of the Arizona desert are the perfect antidote to the dreary winters of their Pacific Northwest home. Each winter, they flee the rain to explore Arizona's deserts, mountains, cities, and small towns. It is the state's unique regional style, Native American cultures, abundance of contemporary art, and, of course, boundless landscapes that keep the duo fascinated by Arizona. Summers find the team researching their other books, including *Frommer's Washington, Frommer's Oregon,* and *Frommer's Seattle & Portland.*

AN INVITATION TO THE READER

In researching this book, we discovered many wonderful places—hotels, restaurants, shops, and more. We're sure you'll find others. Please tell us about them, so we can share the information with your fellow travelers in upcoming editions. If you were disappointed with a recommendation, we'd love to know that, too. Please write to:

Frommer's Phoenix & Scottsdale, 2nd Edition
Wiley Publishing, Inc. • 909 Third Ave. • New York, NY 10022

AN ADDITIONAL NOTE

Please be advised that travel information is subject to change at any time—and this is especially true of prices. We therefore suggest that you write or call ahead for confirmation when making your travel plans. The authors, editors, and publisher cannot be held responsible for the experiences of readers while traveling. Your safety is important to us, however, so we encourage you to stay alert and be aware of your surroundings. Keep a close eye on cameras, purses, and wallets, all favorite targets of thieves and pickpockets.

WHAT THE SYMBOLS MEAN

The following abbreviations are used for credit cards:

AE	American Express	DISC	Discover	V	Visa
DC	Diners Club	MC	MasterCard		

FROMMERS.COM

Now that you have the guidebook to a great trip, visit our website at **www.frommers.com** for travel information on nearly 2,500 destinations. With features updated regularly, we give you instant access to the most current trip-planning information available. At Frommers.com, you'll also find the best prices on airfares, accommodations, and car rentals—and you can even book travel online through our travel booking partners. At Frommers.com, you'll also find the following:

- Online updates to our most popular guidebooks
- Vacation sweepstakes and contest giveaways
- Newsletter highlighting the hottest travel trends
- Online travel message boards with featured travel discussions

The Bes
Scottsda
o

We've chosen wha
Scottsdale, and the V
experiences you wor
ities listed here are
this chapter shoul
you started on yo

1 Frommer
Scottsda

- **Hiking
  the trail
  the m
  steep
  and
  p. 1
- **Str
  T
  p
-

- **Mount**a
  trails of
  and whe
  dirt or a
  are just y
- **Spending**
  there's not
  lie back an
  time for an
  you can us
  (steam room
- **Exploring**
  Phoenix): Th
  from all over
  stroll in the d
- **Driving The**
  winding road f
  This is some o
  Phoenix area, w
  do along the wa
- **Visiting Old Cl**
  (east of Phoenix):
  this is one of the
  that you can still
- **Investigating the**
  (west of Florence):
  this large and unus
  Inscrutable and per

2 The Best Golf Co

- **The Boulders South**
  553-1717): If you've
  beside a massive balan
  hole, you've dreamed
  Course. Jay Morrish's
  through the jumble of
  named. See p. 113.
- **The Gold Course at**
  (Litchfield Park, near Ph
  traditionalist who eschew

desert target courses, you'll want to be sure to reserve a tee time on the Wigwam Resort's Gold Course. This 7,100-yard resort course has long been an Arizona legend. See p. 113.

- **Gold Canyon Golf Resort** (Apache Junction, near Phoenix; ✆ **800/827-5281**): Located east of Phoenix, Gold Canyon offers superb golf at the foot of the Superstition Mountains. The second, third, and fourth holes on the Dinosaur Mountain Course are truly memorable. They play across the foot of Dinosaur Mountain and are rated among the top holes in the state. See p. 113.

- **Troon North Golf Club** (Scottsdale; ✆ **888/TROON-US**): Designed by Tom Weiskopf and Jay Morrish, this semiprivate desert-style course is named for the famous Scottish links that overlook the Firth of Forth and the Firth of Clyde—but that's where the similarities end. Troon North has two 18-hole courses, but the original, known as the Monument Course, is still the favorite. See p. 114.

- **The Tournament Players Club (TPC) of Scottsdale** (Scottsdale; ✆ **888/400-4001**): If you've always dreamed of playing where the pros play, you may want to schedule a visit to the Fairmont Scottsdale Princess and book a tee time on the Stadium Course, which is the site of the PGA Tour's Phoenix Open. See p. 114.

3 The Best Museums

- **Heard Museum** (Phoenix): This is one of the nation's premier museums devoted to Native American cultures. In addition to historical exhibits, a huge kachina doll collection, and an excellent museum store, there are annual exhibits of contemporary Native American art as well as dance performances and demonstrations of traditional skills. See p. 96.

- **Phoenix Art Museum** (Phoenix): This large art museum has acres of wall space and houses an outstanding collection of contemporary art as well as a fascinating exhibit of miniature rooms. See p. 98.

- **Scottsdale Museum of Contemporary Art** (Scottsdale): This is the Phoenix area's newest museum and is noteworthy as much for its bold contemporary architecture as for its wide variety of exhibits. Unlike the majority of area art galleries, this museum eschews cowboy art. See p. 98.

4 The Best Luxury Hotels & Resorts

- **Hyatt Regency Scottsdale** (Scottsdale; ✆ 800/55-HYATT): Contemporary desert architecture, dramatic landscaping, a water playground with its own beach, a staff that's always at the ready to assist you, several good restaurants that aren't over-priced, and even gondola rides—it all adds up to a lot of fun at one of the most smoothly run resorts in Arizona. See p. 42.

- **Marriott's Camelback Inn** (Scottsdale; ✆ 800/24-CAMEL): The Camelback Inn opened in 1936 and today is one of the few Scottsdale resorts that manages to retain an Old Arizona atmosphere while at the same time offering the most modern amenities. A full-service spa caters to those who crave pampering, while two golf courses provide plenty of challenging fairways and greens. See p. 42.

- **The Phoenician** (Scottsdale; ✆ 800/888-8234): This Xanadu of the resort world is brimming with marble, crystal, and works of art, and with staff members seemingly around every corner, the hotel offers its guests impeccable service. Two of the resort's dining rooms are among the finest restaurants in the city, and the views are hard to beat. See p. 43.

- **The Boulders** (Carefree; ✆ 800/553-1717): Taking its name from the massive blocks of eroded granite scattered about the grounds, the Boulders is among the most exclusive and expensive resorts in the state. Pueblo architecture fits seamlessly with the landscape, and the golf course is the most breathtaking in Arizona. See p. 50.

- **The Fairmont Scottsdale Princess** (Scottsdale; ✆ 800/344-4758): The Moorish styling and numerous fountains and waterfalls of this Scottsdale resort create a setting made for romance. Two superb restaurants—one serving Spanish cuisine and one serving gourmet Mexican fare—top it off. See p. 50.

- **Four Seasons Resort Scottsdale at Troon North** (Scottsdale; ✆ 800/332-3442): Located in north Scottsdale, not far from the Boulders, this is one of the state's newest resorts, and it raised the bar on luxury when it opened a few years ago. The setting is dramatic, the accommodations are spacious, and right next door is one of Arizona's top golf courses, the Troon North. See p. 51.

- **Arizona Biltmore Resort & Spa** (Phoenix; ✆ 800/950-0086): Combining discreet service and the architectural styling of Frank Lloyd Wright, the Biltmore has long been one of the most prestigious resorts in the state. This is a thoroughly old-money sort of place, though it continues to keep pace with the times. See p. 53.

- **Royal Palms Hotel and Casitas** (Phoenix; © 800/ 672-6011): With its Mediterranean styling and towering palm trees, this place seems far removed from the glitz that prevails at most area resorts. The Royal Palms is a classic, perfect for romantic getaways, and the 14 designer showcase rooms are among the most dramatic in the valley. See p. 54.

5 The Best Family Resorts

- **Doubletree La Posada Resort** (Scottsdale; © 800/222-TREE): With its waterfalls and swim-through cave, the pool at this Scottsdale resort seems like it ought to be peopled with pirates and castaways. See p. 45.
- **Holiday Inn SunSpree Resort** (Scottsdale; © 800/852-5205): If you happen to have a child who is crazy about trains, this resort, adjacent to the McCormick-Stillman Railroad Park (which has trains to ride, model-railroad exhibits, and a merry-go-round), is the place to stay. The resort itself has big lawns and free meals for kids under 12. See p. 47.
- **Pointe Hilton Squaw Peak Resort** (Phoenix; © 800/876-4683): A water slide, tubing river, and waterfall make the water park here the most family oriented at any resort in the valley. Throw in a miniature-golf course, a video-game room, and a children's program, and your kids will be begging to come back. See p. 58.

6 The Best Restaurants

- **Marquesa** (North Scottsdale; © 480/585-2735): One of the most romantic restaurants in the valley, Marquesa serves a contemporary interpretation of Mediterranean cuisine. See p. 78.
- **Mary Elaine's** (Phoenix; © 480/423-2530): Mary Elaine's is the very height of elegance and sophistication, serving seasonal flavors from its modern French-Mediterranean kitchen. See p. 81.
- **Medizona** (Scottsdale; © 480/947-9500): Merging Southwestern flavors with those of the Mediterranean, this upscale restaurant offers one of the most distinctive menus in the valley. See p. 71.

- **Roaring Fork** (Scottsdale; ℂ 480/947-0795): Roaring Fork's chef, Robert McGrath, has long been one of the most creative chefs in the Phoenix area. At press time, Roaring Fork was planning on moving to a new Scottsdale location, but hopes to re-create the lively atmosphere of its original location. See p. 72.
- **T. Cook's** (Phoenix; ℂ 602/808-0766): There just isn't a more romantic restaurant in the valley. The focal point of the open kitchen is a wood-fired oven that turns out a fabulous spit-roasted chicken. See p. 82.
- **Vincent Guerithault on Camelback** (Phoenix; ℂ 602/224-0225): With its well-balanced blend of Southwestern and European flavors and great lunch values, this is a good place to make your initial foray into the realm of Southwestern cuisine. See p. 83.

7 The Best Swimming Pools

- **Hyatt Regency Scottsdale** (Scottsdale; ℂ 800/55-HYATT): This Scottsdale resort boasts a 10-pool, 2½-acre water playground complete with sand beach, waterfalls, sports pool, lap pool, adult pool, three-story water slide, giant whirlpool, and lots of waterfalls. See p. 42.
- **The Phoenician** (Scottsdale; ℂ 800/888-8234): This system of seven pools is as impressive as the Hyatt's, but has a much more sophisticated air about it. Waterfalls, a water slide, play pools, a lap pool, and the crown jewel—a mother-of-pearl pool (actually opalescent tile)—add up to plenty of aquatic fun. See p. 43.
- **Pointe Hilton Squaw Peak Resort** (Phoenix; ℂ 800/876-4683): There's not just a pool here, there's a River Ranch, with an artificial tubing river, a water slide, and a waterfall pouring into the large, free-form main pool. See p. 58.
- **Pointe Hilton Tapatio Cliffs Resort** (Phoenix; ℂ 800/876-4683): The Falls, a slightly more adult-oriented pool complex than the one at sister property Pointe Hilton Squaw Peak Resort, includes two lagoon pools, a 40-foot waterfall, a 138-foot water slide, and rental cabanas. See p. 58.
- **The Buttes, A Wyndham Resort** (Tempe; ℂ 800/WYND-HAM): A lush stream cascading over desert rocks seems to feed this free-form pool, a desert-oasis fantasy world you won't want to leave. A narrow canal connects the two halves of the pool, and tucked in among the rocks are several whirlpools. See p. 61.

2

Planning Your Trip to Phoenix, Scottsdale & the Valley of the Sun

Time and again, Phoenix, a city named by an early settler from Britain, has lived up to its name. Like the phoenix of ancient mythology, Arizona's capital city rose from its own ashes—in this case, the ruins of an ancient Indian village. While it took nearly a century for this Phoenix to take flight, the city has risen from the dust of the desert to become one of the largest metropolitan areas in the country.

Although the city has had its economic ups and downs, the Phoenix metropolitan area, often referred to as the Valley of the Sun, is currently booming. The Camelback Corridor, which leads through north-central Phoenix, has become the corporate heartland of the city, and shiny glass office towers keep pushing up toward the desert sky. This burgeoning stretch of road has also become a corridor of upscale restaurants and shopping plazas, anchored by the Biltmore Fashion Park, the city's temple of high-end consumerism. Today, Phoenicians flock to this area for both work and play.

Even downtown Phoenix, long abandoned as simply a place to work, has taken on an entirely new look in recent years, and has now positioned itself as the metro area's main sports and entertainment district. Here, you'll find the America West Arena and the Arizona Diamondbacks' Bank One Ballpark (BOB), which is one of the nation's only baseball stadiums with a retractable roof. On days when there are games or concerts scheduled at either of these venues, you can bet that downtown Phoenix will be a lively place. Additionally, the area is home to several performing-arts venues and quite a few attractions, including historic Heritage Square (downtown's only remaining historic block) and, just a little bit north of downtown, the Heard Museum, which focuses on Native American cultures, and the Phoenix Museum of Art.

Phoenix, Scottsdale & the Valley of the Sun

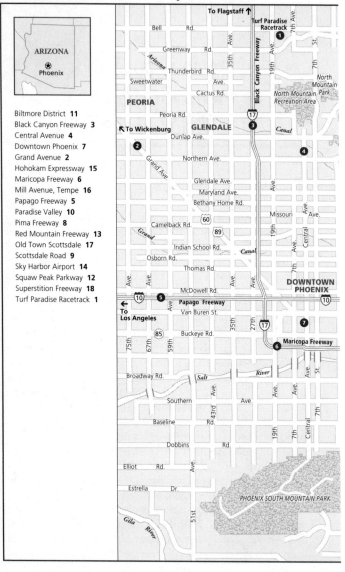

Biltmore District **11**
Black Canyon Freeway **3**
Central Avenue **4**
Downtown Phoenix **7**
Grand Avenue **2**
Hohokam Expressway **15**
Maricopa Freeway **6**
Mill Avenue, Tempe **16**
Papago Freeway **5**
Paradise Valley **10**
Pima Freeway **8**
Red Mountain Freeway **13**
Old Town Scottsdale **17**
Scottsdale Road **9**
Sky Harbor Airport **14**
Squaw Peak Parkway **12**
Superstition Freeway **18**
Turf Paradise Racetrack **1**

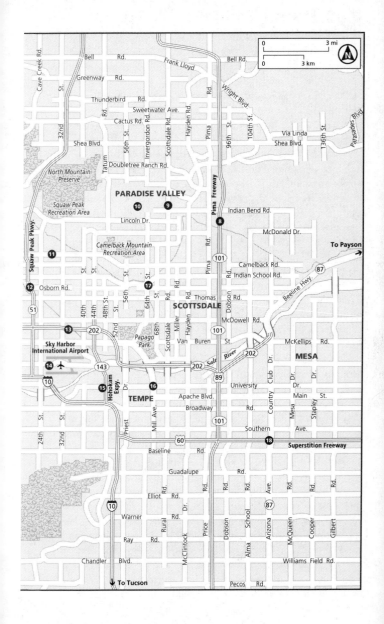

In Scottsdale, luxury resorts sprawl across the landscape, convertibles and SUVs clog the streets, and new golf courses and upscale shopping centers keep springing up like wildflowers after a rainstorm. Until recently, this city billed itself as the West's most Western town, but Scottsdale today is more of a Beverly Hills of the desert than a cow town. The city now sprawls all the way north to Carefree, and it is in north Scottsdale that the valley's newest golf courses and resorts are to be found.

Throughout the metropolitan area, the population is growing at such a rapid pace that an alarm has been raised: Slow down before we become another Los Angeles! Why the phenomenal growth? In large part, it's due to the climate. The 300-plus days of sunshine a year are a powerful attraction, and although summers are blisteringly hot, the mountains—and cooler temperatures—are only 2 hours away. Winter, however, is when the Valley of the Sun truly shines. While most of the country is frozen solid, the valley is usually sunny and warm, making this area the resort capital of the United States. However, with stiff competition from resorts in the Caribbean, Mexico, and Hawaii, Valley of the Sun resorts have had to do a lot of keeping up with the Joneses in recent years. Bigger and splashier pools have been added, and nearly every resort now offers a full-service health spa.

Golf, tennis, and lounging by the pool are only the tip of the iceberg (so to speak) when it comes to winter activities. With the cooler weather comes the cultural season, and between Phoenix and the neighboring cities of Scottsdale, Tempe, and Mesa, there's an impressive array of music, dance, and theater. Scottsdale is also well known as a center of the visual arts, ranking behind only New York and Santa Fe in its concentration of art galleries.

Over the years, Phoenix has both enjoyed the benefits and suffered the problems of rapid urban growth. It has gone from tiny agricultural village to sprawling metropolis in little more than a century. Along the way it has lost some of its past amid urban sprawl and unchecked development; at the same time, it has developed into a city that is quintessentially 21st-century American. Shopping malls, the gathering places of America, are raised to an art form in Phoenix. Luxurious resorts create fantasy worlds of waterfalls and swimming pools. Perhaps it's this willingness to create a new world on top of an old one that attracts people to Phoenix. Then again, maybe it's just all that sunshine.

1 Visitor Information

For visitor center and information desk locations once you arrive, see p. 25.

The city's main visitor center is the **Greater Phoenix Convention & Visitors Bureau** (© 877/225-5749 or 602/254-6500; www.phoenixcvb.com). The **Visitor Information Line** (© 602/252-5588) has recorded information about current events in Phoenix and is updated weekly.

You can do additional research online by visiting the following websites: CitySearch Phoenix (www.phoenix.citysearch.com), which provides a visitors' guide of city essentials; and the Phoenix Area Guide (http://phoenix.areaguides.net), which offers Yellow Pages, White Pages, golf tee times, maps, and more. If you're traveling to Phoenix for business, the accommodations information and meeting planner on the Greater Phoenix Convention & Visitors Bureau website (www.phoenixcvb.com) may be especially helpful. Check out Scottsdale's art scene at www.scottsdalearts.org.

For statewide travel information, contact the **Arizona Office of Tourism,** 2702 N. Third St., Suite 4015, Phoenix, AZ 85007 (© 888/520-3434 or 602/230-7733; www.arizonaguide.com).

2 When to Go

In Phoenix and other parts of the desert, the high season runs from October to mid-May, with the highest hotel rates in effect from January to April. The all-around best times to visit are spring and autumn, when temperatures are cool in the mountains and warm in the desert, but without extremes (although you shouldn't be surprised to get a bit of snow as late as Memorial Day in the mountains). These are also good times to save money—summer rates are in effect at many of the desert resorts in spring and autumn. In spring, you might also catch great wildflower displays, which begin in midspring and extend until April and May. If you happen to be visiting the desert in July or August, be prepared for sudden thunderstorms. These storms often cause flash floods that make many roads briefly impassable. Signs warning motorists not to enter low areas when flooded are meant to be taken very seriously.

Be mindful of the fact that the desert can be cold as well as hot. Although winter is the prime tourist season in Phoenix, night temperatures can be below freezing, and days can sometimes be too cold for sunning or swimming. On the whole, however, winters are positively delightful.

Phoenix's Average Temperatures & Days of Rain

	Jan	Feb	Mar	Apr	May	June	July	Aug	Sept	Oct	Nov	Dec
Avg. High (°F)	65	69	75	84	93	102	105	102	98	88	75	66
Avg. High (°C)	18	21	24	29	34	39	41	39	37	31	24	19
Avg. Low (°F)	38	41	45	52	60	68	78	76	69	57	45	39
Avg. Low (°C)	3	5	7	11	16	20	26	24	21	14	7	4
Days of Rain	4	4	3	2	1	1	4	5	3	3	2	4

PHOENIX & SCOTTSDALE CALENDAR OF EVENTS

January

Tostitos Fiesta Bowl Football Classic, Sun Devil Stadium, Tempe. This college bowl game usually sells out nearly a year in advance. For information, call ℂ **800/635-5748** or 480/350-0900, or go to www.tostitosfiestabowl.com. Early January.

Barrett-Jackson Collector Car Auction, Scottsdale. Immaculately restored classic cars are auctioned off in an event attended by more than 150,000 people. Call ℂ **480/421-6694** for details. Mid-January.

Phoenix Open Golf Tournament, Scottsdale. Prestigious PGA golf tournament at the Tournament Players Club. Call ℂ **602/ 870-4431** for details, or go to www.phoenixopen.com. January 20 to 26, 2003.

February

Parada del Sol Parade and Rodeo, Scottsdale. The state's longest horse-drawn parade, plus a street dance and rodeo. Call ℂ **480/ 990-3179,** or go to www.scottsdalejaycees.com. Early February.

World Championship Hoop Dance Contest, Phoenix. Native American dancers from around the nation take part in this colorful competition held at the Heard Museum. Call ℂ **602/ 252-8840,** or go to www.heard.org. Early February.

O'odham Tash, Casa Grande. One of the largest annual Native American festivals in the country, attracting dozens of tribes and featuring rodeos, arts-and-crafts exhibits, and dance performances. Call ℂ **520/836-4723.** Mid-February.

All-Arabian Horse Show, Scottsdale's Westworld. A celebration of the Arabian horse. Call ℂ **480/515-1500,** or go to www.scottsdaleshow.com. Mid- to late February.

March

Heard Museum Guild Indian Fair, Phoenix. Indian cultural and dance presentations and one of the greatest selections of Native American crafts in the Southwest make this a fascinating festival. Go early to avoid the crowds. Call ✆ **602/252-8848,** or go to www.heard.org. First weekend in March.

Franklin Templeton Tennis Classic, Scottsdale. Top names in men's professional tennis, including the likes of Andre Agassi and Pete Sampras, compete in this tournament at the Fairmont Scottsdale Princess resort. Call ✆ **480/922-0222,** or go to www.scottsdaletennis.com. Early March.

Scottsdale Arts Festival, Scottsdale Mall. This visual and performing arts festival has free concerts, an art show, and children's events. Phone ✆ **800/555-MENU,** or go to www.scottsdale arts.org. Second weekend in March.

National Festival of the West, Scottsdale. A celebration of all things cowboy, from Western movies to music. There's a chuckwagon cook-off, a mountain-man rendezvous, even a cowboy costume contest. Call ✆ **602/996-4387.** March 13 to 16, 2003.

The Countrywide Tradition, Scottsdale. This Senior PGA tournament at Prospector Course at Superstition Mountain Golf & Country Club hosts the big names of days gone by. Call ✆ **480/595-4070,** or go to www.countrywidetradition.com. Late March to early April.

April

Maricopa County Fair, Phoenix. The Arizona State Fairgrounds hosts a midway, agricultural and livestock exhibits, and entertainment. Call ✆ **602/252-0717.** Mid-April.

May

Cinco de Mayo, Phoenix, and other cities. Celebration of the Mexican victory over the French in a famous 1862 battle, complete with food, music, and dancing. Call ✆ **602/279-4669** for details on the festivities in Phoenix. Around May 5.

July

Independence Day. For information on fireworks displays in Phoenix, call ✆ **602/534-FEST.** In other areas, contact the local chamber of commerce. July 4.

October

Arizona State Fair, Phoenix. Rodeos, top-name entertainment, and ethnic food. Call ✆ **602/252-6771,** or go to www.azstatefair.com. Late October.

Annual Cowboy Artists of America Exhibition, Phoenix. The Phoenix Art Museum hosts the most prestigious and best-known Western-art show in the region. Call © **602/257-1222.** Late October.

November

Thunderbird Balloon Classic, Scottsdale. More than 150 hot-air balloons fill the Arizona sky. Call © **602/978-7330.** Early November.

December

Old Town Fall Festival of the Arts, Tempe. Hundreds of artists and artisans set up along Mill Avenue. The festival features free entertainment and plenty of food. Call © **480/967-4877.** Early December.

Pueblo Grande Museum Indian Market, Phoenix. Largest market of its kind in the state, featuring more than 450 Native American artisans. Call © **877/706-4408** or 602/495-0901. Second full weekend in December.

Fiesta Bowl Parade, Phoenix area. Huge, nationally televised parade, featuring floats and marching bands. Call © **800/635-5748,** or go to www.tostitosfiestabowl.com. Late December.

3 Tips for Travelers with Special Needs

FOR TRAVELERS WITH DISABILITIES Many car-rental companies offer hand-controlled cars for drivers with disabilities. Avis can provide such a vehicle at many of its locations with 24-hour advance notice; Hertz requires between 24 and 48 hours of advance notice at most of its locations. **Wheelchair Getaways** (© **800/642-2042;** www.wheelchair-getaways.com) rents specialized vans with wheelchair lifts and other features for travelers with disabilities in about 45 cities across the United States.

Accessible Journeys (© **800/TINGLES** or 610/521-0339; www.accessiblejourneys.com), for slow walkers and wheelchair travelers, offers excursions to the Phoenix area. **The Society for Accessible Travel and Hospitality** (© **212/447-7284;** fax 212/725-8253; www.sath.org) offers a wealth of travel resources for people with all types of disabilities, plus informed recommendations on destinations, access guides, travel agents, tour operators, vehicle rentals, and companion services. Annual membership costs $45 for adults, $30 for seniors and students.

The Healthy Traveler

No matter what time of year it is, the desert sun is strong and bright. Use sunscreen when outdoors—particularly if you're up in the mountains, where the altitude makes sunburn more likely. The bright sun also makes sunglasses a necessity.

Even if you don't feel hot in the desert, the dry air steals moisture from your body, so drink plenty of fluids.

When driving long distances, always carry plenty of drinking water, and, if you're heading off onto dirt roads, bring extra water for your car's radiator as well.

Because the desert is home to poisonous creatures, never stick your hand into holes among the rocks in the desert, look to see where you're going to step before putting your foot down, and avoid turning over rocks and logs.

Mobility International USA (© 541/343-1284; www. miusa.org) publishes *A World of Options,* a book of resources covering everything from biking trips to scuba outfitters, plus a biannual newsletter. Annual membership is $35. ***Open World for Disability and Mature Travel*** magazine, published by the Society for Accessible Travel and Hospitality (see above), is full of good resources and information. A year's subscription is $18 ($35 outside the U.S.). **Travelin' Talk Network** (© 303/232-2979; www. travelintalk.net) operates a website for travelers with disabilities. Each month, members receive an e-mail newsletter with information on discounts, accessible hotels, trip companions, and other tips. A lifetime membership costs $20. The company also operates **www.access-able.com**, which supplies information on trip planning and travel agents.

FOR GAYS & LESBIANS   To get in contact with the Phoenix gay community, contact the **Gay and Lesbian Community Center,** 24 W. Camelback Rd., Suite C (© 602/234-2752; www. phxcenter.org). At the community center and at gay bars around Phoenix, you can pick up various publications such as *Echo* and *Heat Stroke.*

Out and About (© 800/929-2268 or 415/644-8044; www. outandabout.com) offers guidebooks and newsletters packed with solid information on the global gay and lesbian scene.

FOR SENIORS Mention the fact that you're a senior when you first make your travel reservations—most major airlines offer discounts for seniors. Carry photo ID to avail yourself of senior discounts at attractions, at accommodations, and on public transportation.

Members of **AARP** (formerly known as the American Association of Retired Persons), 601 E St. NW, Washington, DC 20049 (© 800/424-3410; www.aarp.org), get discounts on many lodgings, airfares, car rentals, and attractions throughout Arizona. Anyone over 50 can join.

Elderhostel (© 877/426-8056; www.elderhostel.org) arranges study programs for those 55 and over (and a companion of any age). Most courses last 5 to 7 days, and many include airfare, accommodations in university dormitories or modest inns, meals, and tuition. **Grand Circle Travel** (© 800/221-2610 or 617/350-7500; www.gct.com) offers package deals for the 50-plus market, mostly of the tour-bus variety, with free trips thrown in for those who organize groups of 10 or more.

The Mature Traveler (© 800/460-6676; www.themature traveler.com), a monthly newsletter on senior travel, is a valuable resource. It's available by subscription for $30 a year. *The Book of Deals* is a collection of more than 1,000 senior discounts on airlines, lodging, tours, and attractions around the country; it's available for $9.95 by calling © 800/460-6676.

FOR FAMILIES Be sure to check out our suggestions for family-friendly accommodations, dining, and attractions throughout the book.

How to Take Great Trips with Your Kids (The Harvard Common Press) is full of good general travel advice. **Family Travel Network** (www.familytravelnetwork.com) offers travel tips and reviews of family-friendly destinations, vacation deals, and thoughtful features. **Travel with Your Children** (www.travelwithyour kids.com) is a comprehensive site offering sound advice for traveling with children.

4 Getting There

BY PLANE

Phoenix is served by most major airlines, including **Air Canada** (888/247-2262; www.aircanada.ca), **Aero México** (© 800/237-6639; www.aeromexico.com), **Alaska Airlines** (© 800/426-0333;

Insuring a Good, Healthy Trip

If you need information on travel insurance, contact one of the following popular insurers:

- **Access America** (☎ **800/284-8300;** www.accessamerica. com)
- **Travelex Insurance Services** (☎ **800/228-9792;** www. travelex-insurance.com)
- **Travel Guard International** (☎ **800/826-1300;** www.travel guard.com)

  If you require additional medical insurance, try one of the following companies:

- **MEDEX International** (☎ **888/MEDEX-00** or 410/453-6300; fax 410/453-6301; www.medexassist.com)
- **Travel Assistance International** (☎ **800/821-2828** or ☎ 800/ 777-8710; www.travelassistance.com).

---

www.alaskaair.com), **America West** (☎ 800/235-9292; www. americawest.com), **American** (☎ 800/433-7300; www.aa.com), **British Airways** (☎ 800/247-9297; www.british-airways.com), **Continental** (☎ 800/525-0280; www.continental.com), **Delta** (☎ 800/221-1212; www.delta.com), **Frontier** (☎ 800/432-1359; www.flyfrontier.com), **Lufthansa** (☎ 800/645-3880; www. lufthansa.com), **Northwest/KLM** (☎ 800/225-2525; www.nwa. com), **Southwest** (☎ 800/435-9792; www.southwest.com), **United** (☎ 800/241-6522; www.ual.com), and **US Airways** (☎ 800/ 428-4322; www.usairways.com).

TIPS FOR GETTING THE BEST AIRFARE Consolidators, also known as bucket shops, are a good place to find low fares. Consolidators buy seats in bulk from the airlines and then sell them back to the public at prices below even the airlines' discounted rates. Their small boxed ads usually run in the Sunday travel section of newspapers. Before you pay, however, ask for a confirmation number from the consolidator and then call the airline itself to confirm your seat. Be aware that such tickets are usually nonrefundable or rigged with stiff cancellation penalties. And when an airline runs a special deal, you won't always do better with a consolidator.

For discount and last-minute bookings, try **Air 4 Less** (☎ **800/ FLY-FACTS;** www.air4less.com), which can often get you tickets at significantly less than full fare. Other reliable consolidators include **1-800-FLY-CHEAP** (www.1800flycheap.com); **TFI Tours International** (℡ **800/745-8000** or 212/736-1140; www.lowestprice.com), which serves as a clearinghouse for unused seats; and "rebators" such as **Travel Avenue** (℡ **800/333-3335;** www.travelavenue.com), which rebate part of their commissions to you.

GETTING TO AND FROM THE AIRPORT IN PHOENIX

Centrally located 3 miles east of downtown Phoenix, **Sky Harbor International Airport** (℡ **602/273-3300;** www.phxskyharbor.com) has three terminals, with a free 24-hour shuttle bus offering frequent service between them. For lost and found, call ℡ **602/273-3307.**

There are two entrances to the airport. The west entrance can be accessed from either the Squaw Peak Parkway (Ariz. 51) or 24th Street, while the east entrance can be accessed from the Hohokam Expressway (Ariz. 143), which is an extension of 44th Street. If you're headed to downtown Phoenix, leave by way of the 24th Street exit and continue west on Washington Street. If you're headed to Scottsdale, take the 44th Street exit, go north on Ariz. 143 and then east on Ariz. 202 to Ariz. 101 north. For Tempe or Mesa, take the 44th Street exit, go north on Ariz. 143, and then head east on Ariz. 202.

SuperShuttle (℡ **800/BLUE-VAN** or 602/244-9000; www.supershuttle.com) offers 24-hour door-to-door van service between Sky Harbor Airport and resorts, hotels, and homes throughout the valley. Per-person fares average $16 to downtown Scottsdale and $30 to north Scottsdale.

Taxis can be found outside all three terminals and cost only slightly more than shuttle vans. You can call **Discount Cab** (℡ **602/200-2000**) or **Allstate Cab** (℡ **602/275-8888**) to schedule a taxi. A taxi from the airport to downtown Phoenix will cost around $9; to Scottsdale, $25 to $40.

Valley Metro (℡ **602/253-5000;** www.valleymetro.org) provides public bus service throughout the valley, with the Red Line operating between the airport and downtown Phoenix, Tempe, and Mesa. The Red Line runs daily starting between 3 and 5am and continues operating until after midnight. Buses come every fifteen minutes during rush hour and every half hour at off-peak times. The ride from the airport to downtown takes about 20 minutes and costs $1.25. There is no direct bus to Scottsdale, so you would first need to go to Tempe and then transfer to a northbound bus. You can pick up a copy of *The Bus Book,* a guide and route map for the Valley

Metro bus system, at Central Station, at the corner of Central Avenue and Van Buren Street.

BY CAR

The distance to Phoenix from Los Angeles is approximately 369 miles; from San Francisco, 778 miles; from Las Vegas, 287 miles; from Albuquerque, 455 miles; from Santa Fe, 516 miles; and from Salt Lake City, 660 miles

Phoenix is connected to Los Angeles and Tucson by I-10 and to Flagstaff via I-17. If you're headed to Scottsdale, the easiest route is to take the Red Mountain Freeway (Ariz. 202) east to U.S. 101 north. By the time you read this, U.S. 101 should loop all the way around the north side of the valley. The Superstition Freeway (U.S. 60) leads to Tempe, Mesa, and Chandler.

If you're planning to drive through northern Arizona anytime in the winter, bring chains.

5 For International Visitors

See "Fast Facts: Phoenix & Scottsdale," in chapter 3, for additional information.

ENTRY REQUIREMENTS

Immigration law is a hot political issue in the United States these days, and the following requirements may have changed somewhat by the time you plan your trip. Check at any U.S. embassy or consulate for current information and requirements. You can also go to the **U.S. State Department** website at **www.state.gov**.

VISAS   The U.S. State Department has a **Visa Waiver Pilot Program** allowing citizens of certain countries to enter the United States without a visa for stays of up to 90 days. At press time, these countries included Andorra, Australia, Austria, Belgium, Brunei, Denmark, Finland, France, Germany, Iceland, Ireland, Italy, Japan, Liechtenstein, Luxembourg, Monaco, the Netherlands, New Zealand, Norway, Portugal, San Marino, Singapore, Slovenia, Spain, Sweden, Switzerland, the United Kingdom, and Uruguay. Citizens of these countries need only a valid passport and a round-trip air or cruise ticket in their possession upon arrival. If they first enter the United States, they may also visit Mexico, Canada, Bermuda, and/or the Caribbean islands and return to the United States without a visa. Canadian citizens may enter the United States without a visa; they need only proof of residence.

Citizens of all other countries must have (1) a valid passport that expires at least 6 months later than the scheduled end of their visit to the United States, and (2) a tourist visa, which can be obtained without charge from any U.S. consulate.

To get a visa, the traveler must submit a completed application form (either in person or by mail) with a 1½-inch-square photo, and must demonstrate binding ties to a residence abroad. Usually, you can get a visa at once or within 24 hours, but it may take longer during the summer rush from June to August. If you cannot go in person, contact the nearest U.S. embassy or consulate for directions on applying by mail. Your travel agent or airline office may also be able to supply you with visa applications and instructions. The U.S. consulate or embassy that issues your visa determines whether you will receive a multiple- or single-entry visa and any restrictions on the length of your stay.

British subjects can get up-to-date passport and visa information by calling the **U.S. Embassy Visa Information Line** (© 09061/ 500-590) or the **United Kingdom Passport Service** at (© 0870/ 521-0410; www.ukpa.gov.uk).

MEDICAL REQUIREMENTS Unless you're arriving from an area known to be suffering from an epidemic (particularly cholera or yellow fever), inoculations or vaccinations are not required for entry into the United States. If you have a disease that requires treatment with narcotics or syringe-administered medications, carry a valid signed prescription from your physician to allay any suspicions that you may be smuggling narcotics (a serious offense that carries severe penalties in the U.S).

DRIVER'S LICENSES Foreign driver's licenses are usually recognized in the United States, although you may want to get an international driver's license if your home license is not written in English.

CUSTOMS REQUIREMENTS Every visitor over 21 may bring in, free of duty, the following: (1) 1 liter of beer, wine, or hard liquor; (2) 200 cigarettes, 50 cigars (but not from Cuba; an additional 100 cigars may be brought in under your gift exemption), or 4.4 pounds (2kg) of smoking tobacco; and (3) $100 worth of gifts. These exemptions are offered to travelers who spend at least 72 hours in the United States and who have not claimed them within the preceding 6 months. Meat (with the exception of some canned meat products) is prohibited, as are most fruits, vegetables, and plants (including seeds, tropical plants, and the like). Foreign tourists may bring in or take out up to $10,000 in U.S. or foreign currency with no formalities; larger sums must be declared to U.S. Customs on entering or leaving, which includes filing form CM 4790. For specific information regarding U.S. Customs, call your nearest U.S. embassy or consulate, or contact the **U.S. Customs** office at ℰ **202/927-1770** or www.customs.gov/travel/travel.htm.

INSURANCE

Although it's not required of travelers, health insurance is highly recommended. Unlike many European countries, the United States does not usually offer free or low-cost medical care to its citizens or visitors. Doctors and hospitals are expensive and, in most cases, require advance payment or proof of coverage before they render their services. Other policies can cover everything from the loss or theft of your baggage to trip cancellation to the guarantee of bail in case you're arrested. Good policies also cover the costs of an accident, repatriation, or death. In Europe, packages such as **Europ Assistance** are sold by automobile clubs and travel agencies at attractive rates. **Worldwide Assistance Services** (ℰ **800/ 821-2828;** www.worldwideassistance.com) is the agent for Europ Assistance in the United States. See "Insuring A Good, Healthy Trip," above, for other health insurance companies.

Although lack of health insurance may prevent you from being admitted to a hospital in nonemergencies, don't worry about being left on a street corner to die: The American way is to fix you now and bill you later.

MONEY

The U.S. monetary system has a decimal base: one American dollar ($1) = 100 cents (100¢). Bills commonly come in $1 (a "buck"), $5, $10, $20, $50, and $100 denominations (the last two are not welcome when paying for small purchases or taxi fares). Common coins include the penny (1¢), nickel (5¢), dime (10¢), and quarter (25¢). You may come across a 50¢ or $1 coin as well.

Note: The foreign-exchange bureaus so common in many countries are rare in the United States, even at airports. Try to avoid having to change foreign money or traveler's checks not denominated in U.S. dollars. In fact, leave any currency other than U.S. dollars at home.

TRAVELER'S CHECKS   Traveler's checks *denominated in U.S. dollars* are readily accepted at most hotels, motels, restaurants, and large stores, but might not be accepted at small stores or for small purchases. The best place to change traveler's checks is at a bank. Do not bring traveler's checks denominated in other currencies. The traveler's checks that are most widely recognized are **Visa, American Express,** and **Thomas Cook.**

CREDIT CARDS & ATMS   Credit cards are the most widely used form of payment in the United States. Among the most commonly accepted are **Visa** (BarclayCard in Britain), **MasterCard** (EuroCard in mainland Europe, Access in 'Britain, Chargex in Canada), **American Express, Diners Club, Discover,** and **Carte Blanche.** It is strongly recommended that you bring at least one major credit card. You must have a credit or charge card to rent a car, and often you will need one to reserve a flight or a hotel room. There are, however, a handful of stores and restaurants, and even a few guest ranches and B&Bs, that do not take credit cards, so be sure to ask in advance. Most businesses display a sticker near their entrance to let you know which cards they accept. (*Note:* Businesses may require a minimum purchase, usually around $10, to use a credit card.)

You'll find automated teller machines (ATMs) on just about every block in larger cities. You can call ✆ **800/424-7787** for Cirrus/MasterCard locations, or ✆ **800/843-7587** for PLUS/Visa locations. Some ATMs allow you to draw U.S. currency against your bank and credit cards. Check with your bank before leaving home, and remember that you need your personal identification number (PIN) to withdraw money. Most machines accept Visa, MasterCard, and American Express, as well as ATM cards from other U.S. banks. Expect to be charged up to $1 to $1.50 per transaction, however. One way around these fees is to ask for cash back from purchases at grocery stores, which accept ATM cards and don't charge usage fees.

GETTING TO THE U.S.

Airlines with direct or connecting service from London to Phoenix (along with their phone numbers in Great Britain) include: **Air Canada** (✆ 0870/524-7226; www.aircanada.ca), **American** (✆ 0208/572-5555 in London, or 08457/789-789 outside London; www.aa.com), **British Airways** (✆ 0845/773-3377; www.british-airways.com), **Continental** (✆ 0800/776-464; www.continental.com), **Delta** (✆ 0800/414-767; www.delta.com), **Northwest/KLM** (✆ 012/93-502710; www.nwa.com), **United** (✆ 0845/8444-777; www.ual.com), and **US Airways** (✆ 4420/7484-2100; www.usairways.com).

From Canada, there are flights to Phoenix from Toronto on **Air Canada** (℃ 888/247-2262; www.aircanada.ca), **American** (℃ 800/433-7300; www.aa.com), **America West** (℃ 800/235-9292; www.americawest.com), **Delta** (℃ 800/221-1212; www.delta.com), **Northwest** (℃ 800/225-2525; www.nwa.com), **United** (℃ 800/241-6522; www.ual.com), and **US Airways** (℃ 800/428-4322; www.usairways.com).

There are flights to Phoenix from Vancouver on **Alaska Airlines** (℃ 800/426-0333; www.alaskaair.com), **America West** (℃ 800/235-9292; www.americawest.com), **Air Canada** (℃ 888/247-2262; www.aircanada.ca), **Delta** (℃ 800/221-1212; www.delta.com), and **United** (℃ 800/241-6522; www.ual.com).

From New Zealand and Australia, there are flights to Los Angeles on **Qantas** (℃ 13-13-13 in Australia; www.qantas.com.au) and **Air New Zealand** (℃ 0800/737-000 in Auckland; www.airnewzealand.co.nz). Continue on to Phoenix on a regional airline such as **America West** (℃ 800/235-9292; www.americawest.com) or **Southwest** (℃ 800/435-9792; www.southwest.com).

AIRLINE DISCOUNTS   Travelers from overseas can take advantage of the APEX (Advance Purchase Excursion) fares offered by all major U.S. and European carriers. For more money-saving airline advice, see "Getting There," earlier in this chapter.

IMMIGRATION & CUSTOMS CLEARANCE   Visitors arriving by air, no matter what the port of entry, should cultivate patience before setting foot on U.S. soil. Getting through immigration control can take as long as 2 hours on some days, especially summer weekends. This is especially true in the aftermath of the World Trade Center attacks, when security clearances have been considerably beefed up at U.S. airports.

People traveling by air from Canada, Bermuda, and certain countries in the Caribbean can sometimes clear Customs and Immigration at the point of departure, which is much quicker.

GETTING AROUND THE U.S.

For specific information on traveling to Arizona, see "Getting There," earlier in this chapter. For information on getting around Arizona, see "Getting Around," in chapter 3.

BY PLANE   Some large airlines (for example, United and Delta) offer travelers on their transatlantic or transpacific flights special discount tickets under the name **Visit USA,** allowing mostly one-way travel from one U.S. destination to another at very low prices. These discount tickets are not on sale in the United States and must be purchased abroad in conjunction with your international ticket. This system is the best, easiest, and fastest way to see the United States at low cost. Get information well in advance from your travel agent or the office of the airline concerned because the conditions attached to these discount tickets can be changed without advance notice.

BY CAR   Driving is the most cost-effective, convenient, and comfortable way to travel here. The interstate highway system connects cities and towns all over the country, and in addition to these high-speed, limited-access roadways, there's an extensive network of federal, state, and local highways and roads. Driving will give you a lot of flexibility in making—and altering—your itinerary and in allowing you to see off-the-beaten-path destinations that cannot be reached easily by public transportation. You'll also have easy access to inexpensive motels at interstate highway off-ramps.

BY TRAIN   International visitors can buy a **USA Railpass,** good for 15 or 30 days of unlimited travel on **Amtrak** (© **800/ USA-RAIL;** www.amtrak.com). These passes are available through many foreign travel agents. (With a foreign passport, you can also buy passes at staffed Amtrak offices in the U.S, including locations in San Francisco, Los Angeles, Chicago, New York, Miami, Boston, and Washington, D.C.) Reservations are generally required and should be made for each part of your trip as early as possible. Amtrak also offers an **Air/Rail Travel Plan** that allows you to travel by both train and plane; for information, call © **800/437-3441.**

BY BUS   Although bus travel is often the most economical form of transit for short hops between U.S. cities, it can also be slow and uncomfortable—certainly not an option for everyone (particularly when Amtrak, which is far more luxurious, offers similar rates). **Greyhound/Trailways** (© **800/229-9424** or 402/330-8552; www.greyhound.com), the sole nationwide bus line, offers an unlimited-travel **Ameripass/Discovery Pass** for 7 days at $199 to $219, 15 days at $299 to $339, 30 days at $389 to $449, and 60 days at $549 to $629. Passes must be purchased at a Greyhound terminal. Special rates are available for seniors and students.

3

Getting to Know Phoenix, Scottsdale & the Valley of the Sun

This chapter provides an overview of the Phoenix metropolitan area, with plenty of advice on how to get around the city and a list of useful resources, from pharmacy locations to contact information for babysitting.

1 Orientation

VISITOR INFORMATION

You'll find **tourist information desks** in the baggage-claim areas of all three terminals at Sky Harbor Airport. The city's main visitor center is the **Greater Phoenix Convention & Visitors Bureau,** 50 N. Second St. (© **877/225-5749** or 602/254-6500; www.phoenixcvb.com), on the corner of Adams Street in downtown Phoenix. There's also a small visitor center at the Biltmore Fashion Park shopping center, at Camelback Road and 24th Street (© **602/955-1963**).

The **Visitor Information Line** (© **602/252-5588**) has recorded information about current events in Phoenix and is updated weekly.

If you're staying in Scottsdale, you may want to drop by the **Scottsdale Chamber of Commerce and Visitors Center,** 7343 Scottsdale Mall (© **800/877-1117** or 480/945-8481; www. scottsdalecvb.com).

CITY LAYOUT

MAIN ARTERIES & STREETS Over the past decade, the Phoenix area has seen the construction of numerous new freeways, and it is now possible to drive from the airport to Scottsdale by freeway rather than have to deal with stoplights and local traffic. U.S. Loop 101 forms a loop around the east, north, and west sides of the valley, providing freeway access to Scottsdale from I-17 on the north side of Phoenix and from U.S. 60 in Tempe.

I-17 (Black Canyon Fwy.), which connects Phoenix with Flagstaff, is the city's main north-south freeway. This freeway curves to the east just south of downtown (where it is renamed the **Maricopa Fwy.** and merges with I-10). **I-10,** which connects Phoenix with Los Angeles and Tucson, is called the **Papago Freeway** on the west side of the valley and as it passes north of downtown; as it curves around to pass to the west and south of the airport, it merges with I-17 and is renamed the Maricopa Freeway. At Tempe, this freeway curves around to the south and heads out of the valley.

North of the airport, **Ariz. 202 (Red Mountain Fwy.)** heads east from I-10 and passes along the north side of Tempe, providing access to downtown Tempe, Arizona State University, Mesa, and Scottsdale (via U.S. 101). On the east side of the airport, **Ariz. 143 (Hohokam Expressway)** connects Ariz. 202 with I-10.

At the interchange of I-10 and Ariz. 202, northwest of Sky Harbor Airport, **Ariz. 51 (Squaw Peak Fwy.)** heads north through the center of Phoenix and is the best north-south route in the city. This freeway is currently being extended north from Bell Road and by late 2003 or early 2004 will link up with the U.S. Loop 101.

South of the airport off I-10, **U.S. 60 (Superstition Fwy.)** heads east to Tempe, Chandler, Mesa, and Gilbert. **U.S. Loop 101** leads north from U.S. 60 (and Ariz. 202) through Scottsdale and across the north side of Phoenix to connect with I-17. This freeway provides the best route from the airport to the Scottsdale resorts. On the east side of the valley, this highway is called the Pima Freeway.

Secondary highways in the valley include the **Beeline Highway (Ariz. 87),** which starts at the east end of Ariz. 202 (Red Mountain Fwy.) in Mesa and leads to Payson, and **Grand Avenue (U.S. 60),** which starts downtown and leads to Sun City and Wickenburg.

Phoenix and the surrounding cities of Mesa, Tempe, Scottsdale, and Chandler, and even those cities farther out in the valley, are laid out in a grid pattern with major avenues and roads about every mile. For traveling east to west across Phoenix, your best choices (other than the above-mentioned freeways) are Camelback Road, Indian School Road, and McDowell Road. For traveling north and south, 44th Street, 24th Street, and Central Avenue are good choices. Hayden Road is a north-south alternative to Scottsdale Road, which gets jammed at rush hours.

FINDING AN ADDRESS   **Central Avenue,** which runs north to south through downtown Phoenix, is the starting point for all east and west street numbering. **Washington Street** is the starting point for north and south numbering. North-to-south numbered *streets* are to be found on the east side of the city, while north-to-south numbered *avenues* will be found on the west. For the most part, street numbers advance by 100 with each block. Odd-numbered addresses are on the south and east sides of streets, while even-numbered addresses are on north and west sides of streets.

For example, if you're looking for 4454 East Camelback Rd., you'll find it 44 blocks east of Central Avenue between 44th and 45th streets on the north side of the street. If you're looking for 2905 North 35th Ave., you'll find it 35 blocks west of Central Avenue and 29 blocks north of Washington Street on the east side of the street. Just for general reference, Camelback marks the 5000 block north.

STREET MAPS   The street maps handed out by rental-car companies may be good for general navigation around the city, but they are almost useless for finding a particular address if it is not on a major arterial, so as soon as you can, stop in at a minimart and buy a Phoenix map. Unfortunately, you'll probably also have to buy a separate Scottsdale map. Alternatively, if you are a member of AAA, you can get a good Phoenix map before you leave home. You can also get a simple map at the airport tourist information desks or at the downtown visitor center.

NEIGHBORHOODS IN BRIEF

Because of urban sprawl, Phoenix has yielded its importance to an area known as the Valley of the Sun (or just "The Valley"), an area encompassing Phoenix and its metropolitan area of more than 20 cities. Consequently, neighborhoods per se have lost much of their significance as outlying cities have taken on regional importance. Think of the valley's many cities as automobile-oriented neighborhoods. That said, there are some neighborhoods worth noting.

Downtown Phoenix   Roughly bordered by Thomas Road on the north, Buckeye Road on the south, 19th Avenue on the west, and Seventh Street on the east, downtown is primarily a business, financial, and government district, where both the city hall and state capitol are located. Downtown Phoenix is also the valley's prime sports, entertainment, and museum district. The Arizona Diamondbacks play big-league baseball in the **Bank One Ballpark (BOB),** while the Phoenix Suns shoot hoops at the **America West Arena.** Of course, there are also lots of sports bars in the area. There are three major performing-arts venues—the historic **Orpheum Theatre,** the **Symphony Hall,** and the **Herberger Theater Center.** At the Arizona Center shopping and entertainment plaza, there's a huge multiplex movie theater as well as several large bars. Downtown museums include the **Phoenix Museum of History** and the **Arizona Science Center,** both located in Heritage and Science Park. Other area attractions include **Heritage Square** (historic homes), the **Arizona State Capitol Museum,** and the **Arizona Mining & Mineral Museum.** On the northern edge of downtown are the **Heard Museum,** the **Phoenix Central Library** (an architectural gem), and the **Phoenix Art Museum.** Currently, the core of downtown is being referred to as Copper Square in an attempt by the city to give the area a neighborhood identity.

Biltmore District   The Biltmore District, also known as the **Camelback Corridor,** centers along Camelback Road between 24th and 44th streets and is Phoenix's upscale shopping, residential, and business district. The area is characterized by modern office buildings and is anchored by the Arizona Biltmore Hotel and Biltmore Fashion Park shopping mall.

Scottsdale   A separate city of more than 200,000 people, Scottsdale extends from Tempe in the south to Carefree in the north, a distance of more than 20 miles. Scottsdale Road between Indian School Road and Shea Boulevard has long been known as **"Resort Row"** and is home to more than a dozen major resorts. However, as Scottsdale has sprawled ever northward, so, too, have the resorts, and now north Scottsdale has become the center of the resort, shopping, and restaurant scene. Downtown Scottsdale, which consists of Old Town, the Main Street Arts and Antiques District, the Marshall Way Contemporary Arts District, and the Fifth Avenue Shops, is filled with tourist shops, galleries, boutiques, Native American crafts stores, and restaurants.

Tempe   Tempe is the home of Arizona State University and has all the trappings of a university town, which means lots of nightclubs and bars. The center of activity, both day and night, is **Mill Avenue,** which has dozens of interesting shops along a stretch of about 4 blocks. This is one of the few areas in the valley where locals actually walk the streets and hang out at sidewalk cafes. (Old Town Scottsdale often has people on its streets, but few are locals.)

Paradise Valley   If Scottsdale is Phoenix's Beverly Hills, then Paradise Valley is its Bel-Air. The most exclusive community in the valley is almost entirely residential, but you won't see too many of the more lavish homes because they're set on large tracts of land.

Mesa This eastern suburb of Phoenix is the valley's main high-tech area. Large shopping malls, many inexpensive chain motels, and a couple of small museums attract both locals and visitors to Mesa.

Chandler Lying to the south of Tempe, this city has been booming over the past few years. New restaurants have opened, the old downtown has gotten something of a face-lift, and there's a big new mall. This area is of interest primarily to east valley residents.

Glendale Located northwest of downtown Phoenix, Glendale has numerous historic buildings in its downtown. With its dozens of antique and collectible stores, it has become the antiques capital of the valley. The city also has several small museums, including the Bead Museum and Historic Saguaro Ranch.

Carefree & Cave Creek Located about 20 miles north of Old Scottsdale, these two communities represent the Old West and the New West. Carefree is a planned community and home to the prestigious Boulders resort and Santa Fe–style El Pedregal shopping center. Neighboring Cave Creek, on the other hand, plays up its Western heritage in its architecture and preponderance of saloons, steakhouses, and shops selling Western crafts and other gifts.

2 Getting Around
BY CAR

Phoenix and the surrounding cities that together make up the Valley of the Sun sprawl over more than 400 square miles, so if you want to make the best use of your time, it's essential to have a car. Outside downtown Phoenix, there's almost always plenty of free parking wherever you go (although finding a parking space can be time consuming in Old Scottsdale and at some of the more popular malls and shopping plazas). If you want to feel like a local, opt for the ubiquitous valet parking wherever possible (just be sure to keep plenty of small bills on hand for tipping the parking attendants).

Because Phoenix is a major tourist destination, excellent car-rental rates are often available. However, taxes on rentals at Sky Harbor Airport run around 30%, which pretty much negates any deal you might get on your rate. If you book far enough in advance, you might get a compact car for less than $180 per week.

All major rental-car companies have offices at Sky Harbor Airport as well as other locations in the Phoenix area. Among them are the following: **Alamo** (✆ 800/327-9633 or 602/244-0897), **Avis** (✆ 800/331-1212 or 602/273-3222), **Budget** (✆ 800/527-0700 or 602/267-1717), **Dollar** (✆ 800/800-4000 or 866/434-2226), **Enterprise** (✆ 800/736-8222 or 602/225-0588), **Hertz** (✆ 800/654-3131 or 602/267-8822), **National** (✆ 800/227-7368 or 602/275-4771), and **Thrifty** (✆ 800/367-2277 or 602/244-0311).

If you'd like a bit more style while you cruise from resort to golf course to nightclub, call **Rent-a-Vette,** 1215 N. Scottsdale Rd., Tempe (✆ **480/941-3001**), which charges $199 to $249 per day for a Corvette. It also rents Porsche Boxters, Mustang GTs, Jaguars XKAs, Plymouth Prowlers, and Dodge Vipers.

At the rugged end of the car-rental spectrum is **Arizona Jeep Rentals** (✆ **602/674-8469;** www.sedonajeeprentals.com), which rents Jeep Wranglers for $99 for a half day, $129 to $149 for a full day. Special deals are sometimes available. Along with your rental, you can get a trail book and directions for various trails into the desert. For two or more people, this is an economical alternative to doing a Jeep tour.

If a Jeep still doesn't offer enough excitement and wind in your hair, how about a motorcycle? **Western States Motorcycle Rentals & Tours** (✆ **602/943-9030;** www.azmcrent.com) rents Harley-Davidson, BMW, and Suzuki motorcycles for $70 to $125 per day. You must have a valid motorcycle driver's license. In Arizona, you don't have to wear a helmet, so you really can ride with the wind in your hair.

BY PUBLIC TRANSPORTATION

Unfortunately, **Valley Metro** (✆ 602/253-5000; www.valleymetro. maricopa.gov), the Phoenix public bus system, is not very useful to tourists. It's primarily meant to be used by commuters. However, if you decide you want to take the bus, pick up a copy of *The Bus Book* at one of the tourist information desks in the airport (where it's sometimes available), at Central Station at the corner of Central Avenue and Van Buren Street, or at any Frys supermarket. Local bus fare is $1.25; express bus fare is $1.75. A 10-ride ticket book, all-day passes, and monthly passes are available.

Of slightly more value to visitors is the free **Downtown Area Shuttle (DASH),** which provides bus service within the downtown area Monday through Friday from 6:30am to 5:30pm. These buses serve regular stops every 6 to 12 minutes; they're primarily for downtown workers, but attractions along the route include the state capitol, Heritage Square, and the Arizona Center shopping mall. In Tempe, **Free Local Area Shuttle (FLASH)** buses provide a similar service on a loop around Arizona State University. For information on both DASH and FLASH, call ✆ **602/253-5000.**

In Scottsdale, you can ride the **Scottsdale Round Up** (✆ **480/ 312-7696**) shuttle buses between Scottsdale Fashion Square, the Fifth Avenue shops, the Main Street Arts and Antiques district, and the Old Town district. These buses operate between mid-November and late May, Monday through Saturday from 11am to 6pm.

BY TAXI

Because distances in Phoenix are so great, the price of an average taxi ride can be quite high. However, if you don't have your own wheels and the bus isn't running because it's late at night or the weekend, you won't have any choice but to call a cab. **Yellow Cab** (✆ **602/ 252-5252**) charges $3 for the first mile and $1.50 per mile there-after. **Scottsdale Cab** (✆ **480/994-1616**) charges $2 per mile, with a $5 minimum.

 FAST FACTS: Phoenix & Scottsdale

American Express There's an American Express office in Biltmore Fashion Park, 2508 E. Camelback Rd. (✆ **602/ 468-1199**), open Monday through Saturday from 10am to 6pm.

Area Codes The area code in Phoenix is 602. In Scottsdale, Tempe, Mesa, and the east valley, it's 480.

ATM Networks ATMs in Arizona generally use the following systems: Star, Cirrus, PLUS, American Express, MasterCard, and Visa.

Babysitters If your hotel can't recommend or provide a sitter, contact the **Granny Company** (✆ **602/956-4040**).

Business Hours The following are general hours; specific establishments' hours may vary. Banks are open Monday through Friday from 9am to 5pm (some also on Sat 9am–noon). Stores are open Monday through Saturday from 10am to 6pm and Sunday from noon to 5pm (malls usually stay open until 9pm Mon–Sat). Bars generally open around 11am, but are legally allowed to be open Monday through Saturday from 6am to 1am and Sunday from 10am to 1am.

Car Rentals See "Getting Around," above.

Climate See "When to Go," in chapter 2.

Currency Exchange You'll find currency-exchange services in major international airports. There's a **Travelex** office (© 800/287-7362 or 602/275-8767; www.travelex.com) at Sky Harbor Airport in Phoenix. In Phoenix, **Bank of America,** 201 E. Washington St. (© **888/279-3264** or 602/523-2371), will exchange money, as will some of the bank's other branches. Also ask at your hotel desk; some hotels might be able to change major currencies for you.

Dentist Call Dental Referral Service (© **800/510-7765**) for a referral.

Doctor Call the Maricopa County Medical Society (© **602/252-2844**) or the Physician Referral and Resource Line (© **602/230-2273**) for doctor referrals.

Electricity Like Canada, the United States uses 110 to 120 volts AC (60 cycles), compared to 220 to 240 volts AC (50 cycles) in most of Europe, Australia, and New Zealand. If your small appliances use 220 to 240 volts, you'll need a 110-volt transformer and a plug adapter with two flat parallel pins to operate them here. Downward converters that change 220 to 240 volts to 110 to 120 volts are difficult to find in the United States, so bring one with you.

Embassies & Consulates All embassies are located in Washington, D.C. Some consulates are located in major U.S. cities, and most nations have a mission to the United Nations in New York City. If your country isn't listed below, call directory information in Washington, D.C. (© **202/555-1212**), for the number of your national embassy.

The embassy of **Australia** is at 1601 Massachusetts Ave. NW, Washington, DC 20036 (© **202/797-3000;** www.austemb.org). There is no consulate in Arizona; the nearest is at Century Plaza Towers, 2049 Century Park E., 19th Floor, Los Angeles, CA 90067 (© **310/229-4828**).

The embassy of **Canada** is at 501 Pennsylvania Ave. NW, Washington, DC 20001 (© **202/682-1740;** www.canadian embassy.org). The nearest consulate is at 550 S. Hope St., 9th Floor, Los Angeles, CA 90071 (© **213/346-2700**).

The embassy of **Ireland** is at 2234 Massachusetts Ave. NW, Washington, DC 20008 (© **202/462-3939;** www.irelandemb.org).

The nearest consulate is at 44 Montgomery St., Suite 3830, San Francisco, CA 94104 (© 415/392-4214).

The embassy of **New Zealand** is at 37 Observatory Circle NW, Washington, DC 20008 (© 202/328-4800; www.nzemb. org). The nearest consulate is at 12400 Wilshire Blvd., Suite 1150, Los Angeles, CA 90025 (© 310/207-1605).

The embassy of the **United Kingdom** is at 3100 Massachusetts Ave. NW, Washington, DC 20008 (© 202/588-7850; www.britainusa.com). The nearest consulate is at 11766 Wilshire Blvd., Suite 1200, Los Angeles, CA 90025 (© 310/481-0031).

Emergencies Dial © **911** to report a fire, call the police, or get an ambulance. This is a free call (no coins are required at public telephones).

If you encounter serious problems, contact **Traveler's Aid Society International** (© 202/546-1127; www.travelersaid. org) to help direct you to a local branch. This nationwide, nonprofit, social-service organization geared to helping travelers in difficult straits offers services that might include reuniting families separated while traveling, providing food and/or shelter to people stranded without cash, or even emotional counseling.

Eyeglass Repair The **Nationwide Vision Center** has nearly 30 locations around the valley, including 7904 E. Chaparral Rd., Scottsdale (© **480/874-2543**); 4615 E. Thomas Rd., Phoenix (© 602/952-8667); and 933 E. University Dr., Tempe (© **480/966-4992**).

Gasoline (Petrol) Petrol is known as gasoline (or simply "gas") in the United States, and petrol stations are known as both gas stations and service stations. Taxes are already included in the printed price. One U.S. gallon equals 3.8 liters or .85 imperial gallons.

Holidays Banks, government offices, post offices, and many stores, restaurants, and museums are closed on the following legal national holidays: January 1 (New Year's Day), the third Monday in January (Martin Luther King, Jr. Day), the third Monday in February (Presidents' Day, Washington's Birthday), the last Monday in May (Memorial Day), July 4 (Independence Day), the first Monday in September (Labor Day), the second Monday in October (Columbus Day), November 11 (Veterans'

Day/Armistice Day), the fourth Thursday in November (Thanksgiving Day), and December 25 (Christmas). Also, the Tuesday following the first Monday in November is Election Day and is a federal government holiday in presidential-election years (held every 4 years, and next in 2004)

Hospitals The **Good Samaritan Regional Medical Center,** 1111 E. McDowell Rd., Phoenix (✆ **602/239-2000**), is one of the largest hospitals in the valley.

Internet Access If your hotel doesn't provide Internet access, your next best bet is to visit one of the **Kinko's** in the area. There are locations in downtown Phoenix at 201 E. Washington St., Suite 101 (✆ **602/252-4055**); off the Camelback Corridor at 3801 N. Central Ave. (✆ **602/241-9440**); and in Scottsdale just off Indian School Road at 4150 N. Drinkwater Blvd. (✆ **480/946-0500**).

Legal Aid If you are visiting from outside the U.S. and are "pulled over" for a minor infraction (such as speeding), never attempt to pay the fine directly to a police officer; this could be construed as bribery, a much more serious crime. Pay fines by mail, or directly into the hands of the clerk of the court. If accused of a more serious offense, say and do nothing before consulting a lawyer. Here, the burden is on the state to prove a person's guilt beyond a reasonable doubt, and everyone has the right to remain silent, whether he or she is suspected of a crime or actually arrested. Once arrested, a person can make one telephone call to a party of his or her choice. Call your embassy or consulate.

Liquor Laws The legal age for purchase and consumption of alcoholic beverages is 21; proof of age is required and often requested at bars, nightclubs, and restaurants, so it's always a good idea to bring ID when you go out. Beer and wine can often be purchased in supermarkets, but liquor laws vary from state to state. In Arizona, liquor is sold at supermarkets.

Do not carry open containers of alcohol in your car or any public area that isn't zoned for alcohol consumption. The police can, and probably will, fine you on the spot. And nothing will ruin your trip faster than getting a citation for DUI ("driving under the influence"), so don't even think about driving while intoxicated.

Lost Property If you lose something at the airport, call ✆ 602/273-3307; on a bus, call ✆ 602/253-5000.

Mail For International Visitors: If your mail is addressed to a U.S. destination, don't forget to add the five-digit postal code (or ZIP code), after the two-letter abbreviation of the state to which the mail is addressed.

At press time, domestic postage rates were 23¢ for a postcard and 37¢ for a letter. International mail rates vary.

Newspapers & Magazines The *Arizona Republic* is Phoenix's daily newspaper. The Thursday edition has a special section ("The Rep") with schedules of the upcoming week's movie, music, and cultural performances. *New Times* is a free weekly journal with comprehensive listings of cultural events, films, and rock club and concert schedules. The best place to find *New Times* is at corner newspaper boxes in downtown Phoenix, Scottsdale, or Tempe.

Pharmacies Call ☏ **800/WALGREENS** for the Walgreens pharmacy that's nearest you; some are open 24 hours a day.

Police For police emergencies, call ☏ **911.**

Post Office The Phoenix Main Post Office, 4949 E. Van Buren St. (☏ **800/275-8777** or 602/225-3158), is open Monday through Friday from 8:30am to 11:59pm.

Safety See "The Healthy Traveler" and "Insuring A Good, Healthy Trip," both in chapter 2, for insurance and health information.

Don't leave valuables in view in your car, especially when parking in downtown Phoenix. Put anything of value in the trunk, or under the seat if you're driving a hatchback. Take extra precautions after dark in the south-central Phoenix area and downtown. Violent acts of road rage are all too common in Phoenix, so it's a good idea to be polite when driving. Aggressive drivers should be given plenty of room.

If you are bumped from behind, and the situation appears to be suspicious, motion to the other driver to follow you to the nearest police precinct, gas station, or open store.

If someone attempts to rob you or steal your car, do *not* try to resist the thief/carjacker—report the incident to the police department immediately by calling ☏ **911.**

Taxes State sales tax is 5.6% (plus variable local taxes). Hotel room taxes vary considerably by city but are mostly between 10% and 11%. It's in renting a car that you really get pounded: Expect to pay taxes of around 30% when renting a

car at Sky Harbor Airport. You can save around 10% by renting your car at an office outside the airport.

Taxis See "Getting Around," earlier in this chapter

Telephone & Fax Generally, hotel surcharges on long-distance
and local calls are astronomical, so you're usually better off
using a **public pay telephone,** which you'll find clearly marked
in most public buildings and private establishments as well as
on the street. Convenience grocery stores and gas stations
almost always have them. Many supermarkets and convenience stores sell **prepaid calling cards** in denominations up to
$50; these cards can be the least expensive way to call home.
Many public phones at airports now accept American Express,
MasterCard, and Visa. **Local calls** made from public pay phones
in most locales cost either 35¢ or 50¢. Pay phones do not
accept pennies, and few take anything larger than a quarter.

Most long-distance and international calls can be dialed
directly from any phone. **For calls within the United States
and to Canada,** dial 1 followed by the area code and the
seven-digit number. **For other international calls,** dial 011 followed by the country code, city code, and telephone number
of the person you are calling.

Calls to area codes **800, 888, 877,** and **866** are toll-free.
However, calls to numbers in area codes **700** and **900** can be
very expensive—usually 95¢ to $3 or more per minute.

For **reversed-charge** or **collect calls,** and for **person-to-person calls,** dial 0 (zero, not the letter *O*) followed by the area
code and number you want; an operator will then come on
the line, and you should specify that you are calling collect, or
person-to-person, or both. If your operator-assisted call is
international, ask for the overseas operator.

For **local directory assistance** ("information"), dial 411; for
long-distance information, dial 1, then the appropriate area
code and 555-1212.

Time Arizona is in the mountain time zone (MST), but it does
not observe daylight saving time. Consequently, from the first
Sunday in April until the last Sunday in October, there is no
time difference between Arizona and California and other
states on the West Coast.

So, from November through March noon in New York City
(EST) is 11am in Chicago (CST), 10am in Phoenix (MST), 9am in

Los Angeles (PST), 8am in Anchorage (AST), and 7am in Honolulu (HST).

Tipping In hotels, tip **bellhops** at least $1 per bag ($2–$3 if you have a lot of luggage) and tip the **chamber staff** $1 to $2 per day (more if you've left a disaster area to clean up, or if you're traveling with kids and/or pets). Tip the **doorman** or **concierge** only if he or she has provided you with some specific service (for example, calling a cab). Tip the **valet-parking attendant** $1 every time you get your car.

In restaurants, bars, and nightclubs, tip **service staff** 15% to 20% of the check, tip **bartenders** 10% to 15%, tip **checkroom attendants** $1 per garment, and tip **valet-parking attendants** $1 per vehicle. Tip the **doorman** only if he has provided you with some specific service (such as calling a cab for you). Tipping is not expected in cafeterias and fast-food restaurants.

Tip **cab drivers** 15% of the fare.

As for other service personnel, tip **skycaps** (luggage carriers) at airports at least $1 per bag ($2–$3 if you have a lot of luggage) and tip **hairdressers** and **barbers** 15% to 20%.

Toilets Toilets can be found in hotel lobbies, bars, restaurants, museums, department stores, shopping malls, railway and bus stations, and service stations. Large hotels and fast-food restaurants are probably the best bet for good, clean facilities. Note, however, that restaurants and bars in resorts or heavily visited areas may reserve their restrooms for patrons. You can avoid arguments by paying for a cup of coffee or a soft drink, which will qualify you as a patron.

Weather For weather information, call © **800/555-8355.**

4

Where to Stay

Phoenix area has the greatest concentration of resorts in the continental United States. However, even with all the hotel rooms here, sunshine and spring training combine to make it hard to find a room on short notice between February and April (the busiest time of year in the valley). If you're planning to visit during these months, make your reservations as far in advance as possible. Don't forget that in winter, the Phoenix metro area has some of the highest rates in the country. Remember that if a hotel isn't full and isn't expected to be, it's often possible to get a lower rate simply by asking.

With the exception of valet-parking services and parking garages at downtown convention hotels, parking is free at almost all Phoenix hotels. If there is a parking charge, we have noted it. You'll find that all hotels have nonsmoking rooms and all but the cheapest have wheelchair-accessible rooms.

Most resorts offer a variety of weekend, golf, and tennis packages, as well as off-season discounts and corporate rates (which you can often get just by asking). We've given only the official "rack rates," or walk-in rates, below. Hardly anybody pays these prices, however, and there are many ways around them. It always pays to ask about special discounts or packages and to bargain. When booking a room in a chain hotel, compare the rates offered by the hotel's local line with that of the toll-free number. Don't forget your AAA or AARP discounts if you belong to one of these organizations. Remember that business hotels downtown and near the airport often lower their rates on weekends.

If you're looking to save more money, consider traveling during the shoulder seasons of late spring and late summer. Temperatures are not at their midsummer peak nor are room rates at their midwinter highs. If you'll be traveling with children, always ask whether your child will be able to stay for free in your room, and whether there's a limit to the number of children who can stay for free. Also, if you're traveling with your family or another couple, consider a suite. You can pack more people into a suite and thereby reduce your per-person rate.

> *Tips* **A Helping Hand**
>
> Trying to book last-minute accommodations, or simply need help making a reservation? **Greater Phoenix Hotel Reservations** (© 866/231-1114), operated by the Greater Phoenix Convention & Visitors Bureau, can get you low rates at more than 100 hotels and resorts around the valley.

Request a room with a view of the mountains whenever possible. You can overlook a swimming pool anywhere, but some of the main selling points of Phoenix and Scottsdale hotels are the views of Mummy Mountain, Camelback Mountain, and Squaw Peak.

We mention *casitas* in this chapter. Casita, Spanish for little house, is a term used throughout Arizona to refer to large suite-like accommodations. Many are free-standing cottages built in a Pueblo or Spanish Mission style, but some are just regular suites within a hotel complex.

BED-AND-BREAKFASTS While most people dreaming of an Arizona vacation have visions of luxury resorts dancing in their heads, there are also plenty of bed-and-breakfast inns around the valley. **Advance Reservations Inn Arizona/Mi Casa-Su Casa Bed & Breakfast Reservation Service** (© 800/456-0682 or 480/990-0682; www.azres.com) can book you into more than 65 homes in the Phoenix metropolitan area, as can **Arizona Trails Bed & Breakfast Reservation Service** (© 888/799-4284 or 480/837-4284; www.arizonatrails.com), which also books tour and hotel reservations. For a list of some of the best B&Bs in the state, contact the **Arizona Association of Bed & Breakfast Inns** (© 800/284-2589; www.arizona-bed-breakfast.com).

1 Scottsdale

With a dozen or more resorts lined up along Scottsdale Road, Scottsdale is the center of the valley's resort scene. Because Scottsdale is also the valley's prime shopping and dining district, this is the most convenient place to stay if you're here to eat and shop. However, traffic in Scottsdale is bad, the landscape at most resorts is flat (as compared to hillside settings in north Scottsdale), and you don't get much feel for being in the desert.

Phoenix, Scottsdale & the Valley of the Sun Accommodations

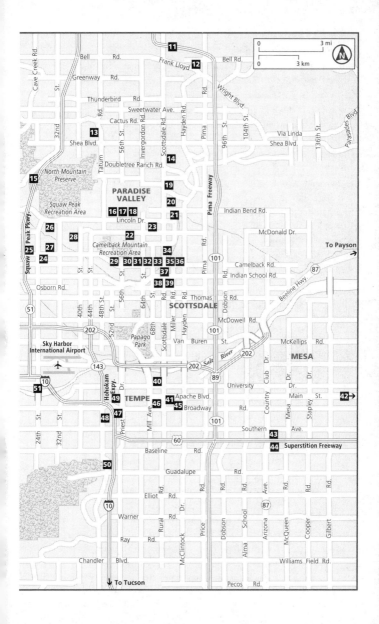

VERY EXPENSIVE

Hyatt Regency Scottsdale ★★★ *Kids* From the colonnades of palm trees to the lobby walls that slide away, this luxurious resort is designed to astonish. A 2½-acre water playground serves as the resort's focal point, and the extravagant complex of 10 swimming pools includes a water slide, a sand beach, a water-volleyball pool, waterfalls, and a huge whirlpool spa. The grounds are planted with hundreds of palm trees that frame the gorgeous views of the distant McDowell Mountains; closer at hand, original works of art have been placed throughout the resort. Guest rooms are luxurious and are designed to reflect the desert location. The top-end Golden Swan restaurant has an unusual sunken waterside terrace (p. 70) while another restaurant provides after-dinner gondola rides. The resort's Hopi Learning Center, staffed by Hopi interpreters, provides a glimpse into Native American culture.

7500 E. Doubletree Ranch Rd., Scottsdale, AZ 85258. (C) **800/55-HYATT** or 480/991-3388. Fax 480/483-5550. www.scottsdale.hyatt.com. 493 units. Jan to mid-May $340–$545 double, from $830 suite and casita; late May to early Sept $190–$250 double, from $410 suite and casita; mid-Sept to Dec $300–$490 double, from $730 suite and casita. AE, DC, DISC, MC, V. **Amenities:** 4 restaurants (New American, Southwestern, Italian); 2 snack bars; 2 lounges; coffee bar; juice bar; 10 pools; 27-hole golf course (with lots of water hazards); 8 tennis courts; health club and spa; Jacuzzi; children's programs; concierge; car-rental desk; business center; shopping arcade; salon; 24-hr. room service; massage; babysitting; laundry service; dry cleaning. *In room:* A/C, TV, dataport, minibar, hair dryer, iron, safe.

Marriott's Camelback Inn ★★★ Set at the foot of Mummy Mountain and overlooking Camelback Mountain, the Camelback Inn, which opened in 1936, is one of the grande dames of the Phoenix hotel scene, abounding in traditional Southwestern character. Over the past few years, the resort has undergone $35 million worth of renovations, which have brought the Camelback Inn into the 21st century and added lots of great amenities. Although the two 18-hole golf courses are the main attractions for many guests, the spa is among the finest in the state, and there's also an extensive pool complex that appeals to families. Guest rooms, which are spread over the sloping grounds, are decorated with Southwestern furnishings and art, and all have balconies or patios. The resort's top restaurant, the Chaparral, has long been a valley favorite.

5402 E. Lincoln Dr., Scottsdale, AZ 85253. (C) **800/24-CAMEL** or 480/948-1700. Fax 480/951-8469. www.camelbackinn.com. 453 units. Jan to early May $429–$460 double, $639–$2,075 suite; mid-May to early Sept $189–$360 double, $235–$1,550 suite; mid-Sept to Dec $360 double, $385–$1,550 suite. AE, DC, DISC, MC, V. Small pets accepted. **Amenities:** 4 restaurants (Continental, Southwestern, healthy, American); 2 snack bars/cafes; lounge; 3 pools; 2 outstanding 18-hole golf courses; pitch-and-putt green; 6 tennis courts; basketball and volleyball courts; exercise room; one of the valley's best full-service spas; 3 Jacuzzis; bike rentals; children's programs and playground; concierge; car-rental desk; business center; salon; room service; massage; babysitting; guest laundry and laundry service; dry cleaning. *In room:* A/C, TV, dataport, minibar, coffeemaker, hair dryer, iron, safe.

Millennium Resort Scottsdale McCormick Ranch ★★ If

you like the heat but not the desert, this resort, with its lakefront setting, is a good choice. Surrounded by green lawns, a golf course, and the water, this relatively small resort strives to convince you that you're not in the desert. The lake (complete with sailboats for guests) is the focal point, but more traditional desert resort activities are available at the two 18-hole golf courses and three tennis courts. The guest rooms all have private balconies or patios, and more than half overlook the lake. If you're here with your family, consider one of the spacious villas. The resort's restaurant serves good Southwestern fare and has a lake view, as does the adjacent lounge.

7401 N. Scottsdale Rd., Scottsdale, AZ 85253-3548. © **800/243-1332** or 480/948-5050. Fax 480/991-5572. www.millenniumhotels.com. 180 units. Feb–Apr $219–$329 double, from $395 suite or villa; May $169–$239 double, from $235 suite or villa; June–Aug $69–$139 double, from $160 suite or villa; Sept–Jan $159–$329 double, from $325 suite or villa. AE, DC, DISC, MC, V. **Amenities:** 2 restaurants (Southwestern); lounge; outdoor pool; 2 18-hole golf courses; 3 tennis courts; volleyball court; pro shop; exercise room; access to nearby health club; Jacuzzi; watersports equipment; bike rentals; concierge; business center; room service; massage; babysitting; laundry service; dry cleaning. *In room:* A/C, TV, dataport, minibar, coffeemaker, hair dryer, iron.

The Phoenician ★★★ *(Kids)* No expense was spared in the construction of this palatial resort, which is situated on 250 acres at the foot of Camelback Mountain, and consequently the Phoenician consistently ranks among the finest resorts in the world. Polished marble and sparkling crystal abound in the lobby, but the view of the valley through a long wall of glass is what commands most guests' attention. Service here is second to none (and can even be overbearing at times). The pool complex, which includes a water slide for the kids, is one of the finest in the state, and the resort's Centre for Well Being offers all the spa pampering anyone could ever need. There are also 27 challenging holes of golf. Mary Elaine's is Phoenix's ultimate special-occasion restaurant, and Windows on the Green is another splendid place to dine (p. 83). Guest rooms, all of which were thoroughly renovated in 2001, are as elaborate as the public areas and have large patios and sunken tubs for two. As luxurious as the rooms are, however, it's questionable whether they warrant the price tag.

6000 E. Camelback Rd., Scottsdale, AZ 85251. ☏ **800/888-8234** or 480/941-8200. Fax 480/947-4311. www.thephoenician.com. 654 units. Late Dec to early May $595 double, from $1,550 suite; mid-May to early June $495 double, from $1,420 suite; mid-June to mid-Sept $245 double, from $700 suite; late Sept to mid-Dec $495 double, from $1,425 suite. AE, DC, DISC, MC, V. Valet parking $22. Pets under 25 lb. accepted. **Amenities:** 3 restaurants (French, Southwestern, Continental/American); 4 snack bars/cafes; lounge; 9 pools; 27-hole golf course; putting green; 12 tennis courts; health club and spa; Jacuzzi; lawn games; bike rentals; children's programs; concierge; car-rental desk; business center; shopping arcade; salon; 24-hr. room service; massage; babysitting; laundry service; dry cleaning. *In room:* A/C, TV, dataport, CD player, minibar, hair dryer, iron, safe.

Renaissance Scottsdale Resort ★★ *Value*   Located behind the upscale Borgata shopping center (which is designed to resemble the Tuscan hill town of San Gimignano), this is an unpretentious yet luxurious boutique resort. Set amid shady lawns, the Renaissance Scottsdale Resort consists of spacious suites designed for those who need plenty of room and comfort. More than 100 of the suites have their own private hot tubs on private patios, and all units are done in Southwestern style. Several excellent restaurants are within walking distance, which makes this a good choice for gourmands who don't want to spend their vacation fighting rush-hour traffic on Scottsdale Road.

6160 N. Scottsdale Rd., Scottsdale, AZ 85253. ☏ **800/HOTELS-1** or 480/991-1414. Fax 480/951-3350. www.renaissancehotels.com. 171 units. Early Jan to May $219–$249 double, $269–$349 suite; June to early Sept $89 double, $109–$129 suite; mid-Sept to Dec $199 double, $249–$309 suite. AE, DC, DISC, MC, V. Pets under 25 lb. accepted ($50 deposit). **Amenities:** Restaurant (Mediterranean); lounge; poolside snack bar; 2 pools; putting green; 4 tennis courts; croquet court; exercise room; access to nearby health club; 2 Jacuzzis; bike rentals; children's programs; concierge; car-rental desk; business center; shopping arcade; room service; massage; babysitting; laundry service; dry cleaning. *In room:* A/C, TV, dataport, minibar, coffeemaker, hair dryer, iron, safe.

Sanctuary on Camelback Mountain ★★★   What was once John Gardiner's Tennis Ranch resort has now been transformed into one of the valley's most visually breathtaking new spa resorts. Located high on the northern flanks of Camelback Mountain, this lushly landscaped property has great views across the valley, especially from the restaurant and lounge. The extremely spacious guest rooms are divided between the more conservative deluxe casitas and the boldly contemporary spa casitas. These latter rooms are the only truly hip lodging option at any of the valley resorts and are designed to compete with the contemporary lodgings in the Palm Springs area. With their dyed-cement floors, kidney-shaped daybeds, and streamline-moderne cabinetry, these units are absolutely stunning (but certainly not for everyone). Some of the huge bathrooms have private outdoor soaking tubs. The spa, which is open only to resort guests and spa members, is one of the prettiest in the valley.

5700 E. McDonald Dr., Paradise Valley, AZ 85253. © **800/245-2051** or 480/948-2100. Fax 480/483-3386. www.sanctuaryoncamelback.com. 98 units. Late Jan to early May, Oct to early Dec, and late Dec $360–$555 double, from $510 casita; mid-May to mid-June $280–$455 double, from $430 casita; late June to Sept and early to mid-Dec $135–$240 double, from $210 casita. AE, DC, DISC, MC, V. Pets accepted. **Amenities:** 2 restaurants (New American, spa cuisine); lounge; 3 pools; 5 tennis courts; fitness center; full-service spa; Jacuzzi; concierge; business center; room service; massage; babysitting; laundry service; dry cleaning. *In room:* A/C, TV, dataport, minibar, coffeemaker, hair dryer, iron.

The Sunburst Resort ⭐⭐ *Value*   An exceptional location in the heart of the Scottsdale shopping district, a dramatic Southwestern styling (the focal point of the lobby is a massive sandstone fireplace), and a small but well-designed pool area are the primary appeals of this resort. Set in a lushly planted courtyard are a small lagoon-style pool, complete with sand beach and short water slide, and a second pool with waterfalls. An artificial stream and fake sandstone ruins all add up to a fun desert fantasy landscape (although not on the grand scale to be found at some area resorts). The comfortable guest rooms are decorated in new "Old West" style, with cowhide prints and peeled log furnishings; French doors open onto patios.

4925 N. Scottsdale Rd., Scottsdale, AZ 85251. © **800/528-7867** or 480/945-7666. Fax 480/946-4056. www.sunburstresort.com. 210 units. Jan to mid-May $189–$259 double, $395–$750 suite; late May to early Sept $89–$119 double, $295–$500 suite; mid-Sept to Dec $189–$219 double, $350–$600 suite. AE, DC, DISC, MC, V. **Amenities:** Restaurant (Southwestern/New American); lounge; snack bar; 2 pools; exercise room; access to nearby health club; Jacuzzi; summer children's programs; concierge; car-rental desk; business center; room service; massage; babysitting; laundry service; dry cleaning. *In room:* A/C, TV, dataport, minibar, coffeemaker, hair dryer, iron.

EXPENSIVE

Doubletree La Posada Resort ⭐⭐ *Kids*   If you prefer to spend your time by the pool rather than on the fairways, La Posada is a great choice, especially if you have the kids along. The pool here, which has a view of Camelback Mountain, covers half an acre and features its own two-story waterfall that cascades over artificial boulders. Connecting the two halves of the pool is a swim-through grotto complete with bar/cafe (and exercise room). Mission Revival architecture prevails throughout the resort. Guest rooms are larger than average and have tiled bathrooms with double vanities.

4949 E. Lincoln Dr., Scottsdale, AZ 85253. ✆ **800/222-TREE** or 602/952-0420. Fax 602/840-8576. www.doubletreelaposada.com. 262 units. Mid-Sept to mid-May $140–$189 double, $400–$550 suite; late May to early Sept $79–$112 double, $400–$550 suite. AE, DC, DISC, MC, V. Pets accepted. **Amenities:** Restaurant (Southwestern); snack bar; 2 lounges; 2 pools; 2 putting greens; 6 tennis courts; 2 racquetball courts; volleyball court; tennis pro shop; exercise room; spa; 4 Jacuzzis; sauna; bike rentals; concierge; car-rental desk; room service; massage; laundry service; dry cleaning. *In room:* A/C, TV, dataport, minibar, fridge, coffeemaker, hair dryer, iron.

Doubletree Paradise Valley Resort ⋆⋆ *Value*

With its low-rise design and textured-block construction, this resort bows to the pioneering architectural style of Frank Lloyd Wright, and thus stands out from comparable resorts in the area. Built around several courtyards containing swimming pools, bubbling fountains, and gardens with desert landscaping, the property has the look and feel of the nearby Hyatt Regency Scottsdale (although on a less grandiose scale). Mature palm trees lend a sort of Moorish feel to the grounds and cast fanciful shadows in the gardens. Accommodations have a very contemporary feel, with lots of blond wood and, in some cases, high ceilings that make the rooms feel particularly spacious. With its distinctive styling and convenient location, this is an excellent choice.

5401 N. Scottsdale Rd., Scottsdale, AZ 85250. ✆ **800/222-TREE** or 480/947-5400. Fax 480/481-0209. www.doubletreehotels.com. 387 units. Jan–Mar $179–$259 double, from $259 suite; Apr and Sept–Dec $99–$169 double, from $199 suite; May–Aug $65–$119 double, from $159 suite. AE, DC, DISC, MC, V. **Amenities:** 2 restaurants (New American, steakhouse); lounge with live music; snack bar; 2 outdoor pools; putting green; 2 tennis courts; 2 racquetball courts; exercise room; 2 Jacuzzis; saunas; concierge; car-rental desk; business center; room service; massage; babysitting; laundry service; dry cleaning. *In room:* A/C, TV, dataport, minibar, coffeemaker, hair dryer, iron.

Embassy Suites Phoenix/Scottsdale ⋆

While cities from New York to San Francisco are busy opening chic and stylishly contemporary hotels as fast as they can, the Valley of the Sun has nearly missed the boat completely. This hotel, however, is one of the area's few exceptions and will appeal to young, hip travelers. As soon as you see the dyed concrete floor and unusual wall sculpture in the lobby, you'll know that this is not your standard business hotel. It will be difficult to take your eyes off the views across Stonecreek Golf Course to Camelback Mountain, Mummy Mountain, and Squaw Peak, and those views just get better the higher up you go (be sure to ask for a room on the south side of an upper floor). Keep in mind that this is an all-suite property; the two-room accommodations are very spacious and come complete with galley kitchens.

4415 E. Paradise Village Pkwy. S., Phoenix, AZ 85032. ℂ **800/EMBASSY** or 602/765-5800. Fax 602/765-5890. www.embassysuitesaz.com. 270 units. Jan–Apr $199–$219 double; May $169–$189 double; June to mid-Sept $89 double; late Sept to Dec $189–$209 double. Rates include full breakfast. AE, DC, DISC, MC, V. **Amenities:** Restaurant (American); lounge; complimentary cocktails; small outdoor pool; exercise room; access to nearby health club; Jacuzzi; concierge; car-rental desk; business center; room service; coin-op laundry; laundry service; dry cleaning. *In room:* A/C, TV, dataport, kitchenette, minibar, coffeemaker, hair dryer, iron, safe.

Holiday Inn SunSpree Resort ★★ (Kids)   Long one of the valley's best resort deals, the SunSpree has been upgrading over the past few years—and its rates seem to be creeping up. Still, compared to other area options, it is relatively economical. Situated on 16 acres amid wide expanses of lawn, the SunSpree may not be as luxurious as other area resorts, but it is a good choice for families (the adjacent McCormick-Stillman Railroad Park is a big hit with kids). Guests can golf at the adjacent Scottsdale Silverado Golf Club, while non-golfers can avail themselves of many other recreational options. Guest rooms have a plush feel that belies the reasonable rates. Ask for a room with a mountain view or a lakeside unit with patio.

7601 E. Indian Bend Rd., Scottsdale, AZ 85250. ℂ **800/852-5205** or 480/991-2400. Fax 480/998-2261. www.arizonaguide.com/sunspree. 200 units. Jan to early Apr $139–$159 double; mid-Sept to Dec and mid-Apr to mid-May $115–$135 double; late May to early Sept $59–$79 double. AE, DC, DISC, MC, V. **Amenities:** Restaurant (New American); lounge; snack bar; 2 pools; 18-hole golf course; 2 tennis courts; volleyball court; lawn games; exercise room; Jacuzzi; bike rentals; room service; coin-op laundry; dry cleaning. *In room:* A/C, TV, dataport, fridge, coffeemaker, hair dryer, iron, safe.

Marriott's Mountain Shadows Resort & Golf Club ★★ (Value) Located across the road from Marriott's Camelback Inn, Mountain Shadows has a much more casual atmosphere than its sister property. Built in the late 1950s and somewhat dated architecturally, this resort is well maintained and will appeal to anyone looking for a good value and an informal setting. While an 18-hole executive course keeps most guests happy, guests also have access to the Camelback Inn's two golf courses, as well as that resort's superb spa. Standard rooms have high ceilings, wet bars, king-size beds, and balconies; the units in the Palm section offer the best views of the mountain. The rooms around the main pool, although large, can be a bit noisy during spring break and other times of year that attract families.

5641 E. Lincoln Dr., Scottsdale, AZ 85253. ℂ **800/228-9290** or 480/948-7111. Fax 480/951-5430. www.mountainshadows.net. 337 units. Early Jan to early May $219–$259 double, $259–$699 suite; mid-May to early Sept $89–$179 double, $125–$350 suite; mid-Sept to Dec $189 double, $259–$659 suite. AE, DC, DISC,

MC, V. Small pets accepted. **Amenities:** 3 restaurants (seafood, Southwestern, American); snack bar; lounge; 3 pools; 18-hole executive golf course; 8 tennis courts; volleyball court; exercise room; spa; 2 Jacuzzis; saunas; concierge; car-rental desk; pro shops; room service; coin-op laundry; laundry service; dry cleaning. *In room:* A/C, TV, dataport, fridge, coffeemaker, hair dryer, iron, safe.

Radisson Resort Scottsdale ★★   With its green lawns, orange trees, and oleanders, this resort doesn't exactly feel Southwestern, despite the attractive new flagstone facade on the front of the main building. However, if a lush landscape and a conservative atmosphere are what you're looking for, this is a good bet. Most guests are attracted by the resort's 21 tennis courts or the two traditional 18-hole golf courses at the adjacent McCormick Ranch Golf Club (which, however, are not among the valley's top courses). Also featured on the property are a large Japanese-style health spa and a pool that's twice normal Olympic size (although the poolside patio seems designed more for conventioneers than for vacationers). Most guest rooms are large and have private patios; the golf-course rooms, with views of the McDowell Mountains, are our favorites.

7171 N. Scottsdale Rd., Scottsdale, AZ 85253. ✆ **800/333-3333** or 480/991-3800. Fax 480/948-1381. www.radisson.com/scottsdaleaz. 318 units. Mid-Jan to mid-Apr $179–$289 double, from $229 suite; late Apr to early June $119–$229 double, from $129 suite; mid-June to early Sept $79–$149 double, from $129 suite; mid-Sept to early Jan $119–$229 double, from $209 suite. AE, DC, DISC, MC, V. **Amenities:** 2 restaurants (New American, Asian); lounge; snack bar; patisserie; 3 pools; 2 18-hole golf courses; 21 tennis courts; health club and full-service spa; Jacuzzi; concierge; car-rental desk; business center; pro shop; salon; room service; massage; coin-op laundry; laundry service; dry cleaning. *In room:* A/C, TV, dataport, minibar, coffeemaker, hair dryer, iron.

MODERATE

Hacienda Resort *(Finds)*   Don't be taken in by the name; this little place is hardly a resort, but it is a well-placed, well-priced getaway spot with the look and feel of updated 1960s apartments. Funky and hip are the watchwords here, although the hipness is concentrated mostly in the tiny lobby. The inn's grassy little courtyard, which has a small pool and a hot tub, is set off from busy Camelback Road by a brick wall that gives the complex a private, residential feel. Rooms are fairly well maintained and range from big to huge. Although the bathrooms are small, most guest rooms have full kitchens. Within just a few blocks are lots of nightclubs, great restaurants, and excellent shopping. A good choice for younger travelers.

7320 E. Camelback Rd., Scottsdale, AZ 85251. ✆ **480/994-4170.** Fax 480/994-9387. www.haciendaresort.com. 22 units. $70–$180 double. AE, DISC,

MC, V. Pets accepted ($15 per night). **Amenities:** Small outdoor pool; coin-op laundry. *In room:* A/C, TV, dataport, kitchenette, fridge, coffeemaker, hair dryer, iron.

Old Town Hotel and Conference Center ⟨⟩   Guest rooms at this low-rise hotel are fairly small (as are the bathrooms), but the location—right on the beautifully landscaped Scottsdale Civic Center Mall (a park, not a shopping center)—is very appealing. The Scottsdale Center for the Arts is just across the mall, and you're only a block away from Old Town Scottsdale and 2 blocks from the art-gallery district. The best units are those opening onto the mall—be sure to ask for one. The hotel's dining room is a very economical steakhouse overlooking the green lawns of the mall.

7353 E. Indian School Rd., Scottsdale, AZ 85251-3942. ℭ **800/695-6995** or 480/994-9203. Fax 480/941-2567. www.oldtownhotelscottsdale.com. 206 units. Jan to mid-Apr $189 double; late Apr to May $129 double; June to early Sept $89 double; mid-Sept to Dec $129 double. Rates include full breakfast. AE, DC, DISC, MC, V. Pets accepted. **Amenities:** Restaurant (steakhouse); lounge; small outdoor pool; putting green; tennis court; access to nearby health club; Jacuzzi; bike rentals; concierge; car-rental desk; business center; courtesy shopping shuttle; babysitting; laundry service; dry cleaning. *In room:* A/C, TV, dataport, coffeemaker, hair dryer, iron.

INEXPENSIVE

Despite the high-priced real estate, Scottsdale does have a few relatively inexpensive chain motels, although during the winter season, prices are higher than you'd expect. The rates given here are for the high season. The **Days Inn–Scottsdale/Fashion Square Resort,** 4710 N. Scottsdale Rd. (ℭ **480/947-5411**), charges $79 to $165 for a double. **Motel 6–Scottsdale,** 6848 E. Camelback Rd. (ℭ **480/946-2280**), offers doubles for $66 to $70. **Rodeway Inn–Phoenix/Scottsdale,** 7110 E. Indian School Rd. (ℭ **480/946-3456**), has rates of $99 to $109 double.

Econo Lodge Scottsdale *⟨Value*   For convenience and price, this motel can't be beat (at least not in Scottsdale). Located at the west end of the Fifth Avenue shopping district, the Econo Lodge is within walking distance of some of the best shopping and dining in Scottsdale. The three-story building is arranged around a central courtyard, where you'll find the small pool. Guest rooms are large and have been fairly recently renovated.

6935 Fifth Ave., Scottsdale, AZ 85251. ℭ **800/528-7396** or 480/994-9461. Fax 480/947-1695. www.econolodge.com. 92 units. Jan to early Apr $79–$109 double; mid-Apr to early Sept $49–$79 double; mid-Sept to Dec $59–$89 double. Rates include continental breakfast. AE, DC, DISC, MC, V. **Amenities:** Small outdoor pool; exercise room; coin-op laundry. *In room:* A/C, TV, fridge, coffeemaker, hair dryer, iron.

2 North Scottsdale, Carefree & Cave Creek

North Scottsdale is the brave new world for Valley of the Sun resorts. Situated at least a 30-minute drive from downtown Scottsdale, this area may be too far out of the mainstream for many visitors. However, if you're willing to stay this far north of all the action, what you'll get is the newest resorts, the most spectacular hillside settings, and the best golf courses.

VERY EXPENSIVE

The Boulders 𝄐𝄐𝄐   Set amid a jumble of giant boulders 45 minutes north of Scottsdale, this prestigious golf resort, more than any other in the Phoenix area, epitomizes the Southwest aesthetic. Adobe buildings blend unobtrusively into the desert, as do the two acclaimed golf courses. If you can tear yourself away from the fairways, you can relax around the pool, play tennis, take advantage of the new Golden Door Spa, or even try your hand at rock climbing. The lobby is in a Santa Fe–style building with tree-trunk pillars and a flagstone floor, and the guest rooms continue the pueblo styling with stucco walls, beehive fireplaces, and beamed ceilings. For the best views, ask for one of the second-floor units. Bathrooms are large and luxuriously appointed, with tubs for two and separate showers. In addition to the upscale on-site restaurants, there are several other dining options at the adjacent El Pedregal Festival Marketplace.

34631 N. Tom Darlington Dr. (P.O. Box 2090), Carefree, AZ 85377. ℭ **800/ 553-1717,** 800/WYNDHAM, or 480/488-9009. Fax 480/488-4118. www.wyndham. com/luxury. 210 units. Late Dec to mid-May $495–$625 double, from $595 villa; late May to early Sept $205 double, from $245 villa; mid-Sept to early Dec $495 double, from $595 villa; mid-Dec $290 double, from $350 villa (plus nightly service charge of $27–$31, year-round). AE, DC, DISC, MC, V. Pets accepted ($100). **Amenities:** 7 restaurants (New American, Southwestern, American, spa cuisine); lounge; 4 pools; 2 18-hole golf courses; pro shop; 8 tennis courts; exercise room; full-service spa; 3 Jacuzzis; bike rentals; children's programs; concierge; business center; shopping arcade; salon; room service; massage; babysitting; laundry service; dry cleaning. In room: A/C, TV, dataport, minibar, coffeemaker, hair dryer, iron, safe.

The Fairmont Scottsdale Princess 𝄐𝄐𝄐   With its royal palms, tiled fountains, and waterfalls, the Princess is a modern rendition of a Moorish palace and offers an exotic atmosphere unmatched by any other valley resort. It's also home to the Phoenix Open golf tournament and the city's top tennis tournament, which means the two golf courses here are superb and the courts are top-notch. There's also the Willow Stream spa and a water playground complete with the two longest resort water slides in Arizona. This resort, located a 20-minute drive north of Old Town Scottsdale, will delight anyone in search of a romantic hideaway, while families will enjoy both the water playground and the pond where kids can go fishing. The decor of the guest rooms is elegant Southwestern, and all units have private balconies. The spacious bathrooms have double vanities and separate showers and tubs. The Marquesa serves superb Spanish cuisine, while upscale Mexican food and mariachis are the specialties at La Hacienda (p. 78).

7575 E. Princess Dr., Scottsdale, AZ 85255. © **800/344-4758** or 480/585-4848. Fax 480/585-0086. www.fairmont.com. 650 units. Jan to mid-Apr $359–$589 double, $569–$3,800 suite; late Apr to May and mid-Sept to Dec $249–$409 double, $439–$3,800 suite; June to early Sept $169–$319 double, $369–$3,800 suite. AE, DC, DISC, MC, V. Pets accepted. **Amenities:** 4 restaurants (Spanish, Mexican, steakhouse, American); 3 lounges; 4 pools; 2 18-hole golf courses; 7 tennis courts; exercise room; full-service spa; Jacuzzi; bike rentals; concierge; car-rental desk; business center; golf and tennis pro shops; shopping arcade; salon; 24-hr. room service; massage; babysitting; laundry service; dry cleaning. *In room:* A/C, TV, dataport, minibar, coffeemaker, hair dryer, iron, safe.

Four Seasons Resort Scottsdale at Troon North 🐾🐾🐾

Located in the foothills of north Scottsdale, adjacent to and with privileges at the Troon North golf course (one of the state's most highly acclaimed courses), the Four Seasons has been working hard to knock the nearby Boulders resort from its pinnacle. With casita accommodations scattered across a boulder-strewn hillside, the Four Seasons boasts one of the most dramatic settings in the valley. Likewise, the guest rooms and suites are among the most lavish you'll find in Arizona. If you can afford it, opt for one with a private plunge pool and an outdoor shower—a luxury usually found only in tropical resorts. With three restaurants on the premises, it's easy to forget how far out of the Scottsdale mainstream this place is.

10600 E. Crescent Moon Dr., Scottsdale, AZ 85255. © **800/332-3442** or 480/515-5700. Fax 480/515-5599. www.fourseasons.com. 210 units. Jan to early May $500–$650 double, $795–$4,000 suite; mid-May to mid-June and mid-Sept to late Dec $445–$545 double, $795–$4,000 suite; late June to early Sept $185–275 double, $375–$2,000 suite. AE, DC, DISC, MC, V. Pets accepted. **Amenities:** 3 restaurants (Italian, steakhouse, Mexican); lounge; large 2-level pool plus children's pool; 2 18-hole golf courses; 4 tennis courts; large exercise room; spa; Jacuzzi; children's programs; concierge; car-rental desk; business center; salon; 24-hr. room service; massage; babysitting; laundry service; dry cleaning. *In room:* A/C, TV/VCR, dataport, minibar, coffeemaker, hair dryer, iron, safe.

EXPENSIVE

Copperwynd Country Club & Inn ✦✦ *Value* Although it's a long way out, this boutique hotel, high on a ridge overlooking the town of Fountain Hills, is one of the most luxurious in the area. The property, part of an exclusive country-club community, is surrounded by a rugged desert landscape, which is one of the reasons we like this place so much: You know you're in the desert when you stay here. Although there's no golf course on the premises, there are several nearby. Instead of golf, the resort emphasizes tennis and also has an impressive health club and small spa. The views are among the finest in the valley, and the Jacuzzi tucked into a rocky hillside is as romantic as they come. All guest rooms have great views and feature a sort of European deluxe decor. Balconies provide plenty of room for taking in the vista. There's an excellent restaurant on the premises, so the distance from town isn't as significant as it might otherwise be.

13225 N. Eagle Ridge Dr., Fountain Hills, AZ 85268. ✆ **877/707-7760** or 480/333-1900. www.copperwynd.com. 40 units. Late Dec to mid-Apr $249–$425 double, $1,000–$1,600 villa; late Apr to mid-May and late Sept to mid-Dec $179–$249 double, $800–$1,000 villa; late May to mid-Sept $129–$189 double, $400–$500 villa. AE, DC, DISC, MC, V. Small pets accepted ($50). **Amenities:** 2 restaurants (New American, American); lounge; juice bar; 2 pools; 9 tennis courts; health club and full-service spa; Jacuzzi; children's programs; game room; concierge; pro shop; salon; room service; massage; babysitting; laundry service; dry cleaning. *In room:* A/C, TV, dataport, fridge, coffeemaker, hair dryer, iron, safe.

Scottsdale Marriott at McDowell Mountains ✦ This all-suite hotel, not far from the Scottsdale Princess, overlooks the Tournament Players Club (TPC) Desert Course, and while this may not be the TPC's main course, it manages to give the hotel a very resortlike feel. The suites feature luxurious bathrooms done in marble and granite; some units have balconies. Those rooms overlooking the golf course are worth requesting, although there are also good views of the McDowell Mountains from some units. The location, just off the U.S. 101 Loop freeway and midway between Carefree and Old Scottsdale, makes this a surprisingly convenient choice.

16770 N. Perimeter Dr., Scottsdale, AZ 85260. ✆ **800/228-9290** or 480/502-3836. Fax 480/502-0653. www.marriottscottsdale.com. 270 units. Jan to mid-May $260–$340 double; late May to early Sept $150 double; mid-Sept to Dec $240 double. AE, DC, DISC, MC, V. **Amenities:** Restaurant (Mediterranean); lounge; poolside snack bar; pool; adjacent 18-hole golf course; exercise room; Jacuzzi; saunas; concierge; car-rental desk; business center; room service; laundry service; dry cleaning. *In room:* A/C, TV, dataport, minibar, coffeemaker, hair dryer, iron.

3 Central Phoenix & the Camelback Corridor

This area is the heart of the upscale Phoenix shopping and restaurant scene and is home to the Arizona Biltmore, one of the most prestigious resorts in the city. Old money and new money rub shoulders along the avenues here, and valet parking is de rigueur. Located roughly midway between Old Scottsdale and downtown Phoenix, this area is a good bet for those intending to split their time between the downtown Phoenix cultural and sports district and the world-class shopping and dining in Scottsdale. The area has only one golf resort, but boasts a couple of smaller boutique hotels with loads of Arizona character.

VERY EXPENSIVE

Arizona Biltmore Resort & Spa 🎖🎖🎖 *Kids*   For timeless elegance, a prime location, and historic character, no other resort in the valley can touch the Arizona Biltmore. For decades, this has been the favored Phoenix address of celebrities and politicians, and the distinctive cast-cement blocks designed by Frank Lloyd Wright make it one of the valley's architectural gems. While the two golf courses and expansive spa are the main draws for many guests, the children's activities center also makes this a popular choice for families. Of the several different styles of accommodations, the "resort rooms" are quite comfortable and come with balconies or patios. Those rooms in the Arizona Wing are also good choices. The villa suites are the most spacious and luxurious of all. Afternoon tea, a Phoenix institution, is served in the lobby. In Wright's, the main dining room, guests dine amid the handiwork of Frank Lloyd Wright.

2400 E. Missouri Ave., Phoenix, AZ 85016. ⓒ **800/950-0086** or 602/955-6600. Fax 602/954-2571. www.arizonabiltmore.com. 730 units. Jan to early May $350–$550 double, from $675 suite; mid-May to late May and mid-Sept to Dec $310–$465 double, from $550 suite; June to early Sept $175–$260 double, from $340 suite (plus daily service fee of $12, year-round). AE, DC, DISC, MC, V. Pets under 20 lb. accepted in cottage rooms ($250 deposit, $50 nonrefundable). **Amenities:** 3 restaurants (New American, Southwestern, American); snack bar; lounge; 8 pools (with a water slide and rental cabanas); 2 18-hole golf courses plus 18-hole putting course; 7 tennis courts; lawn games; health club and full-service spa; 2 Jacuzzis; saunas; bike rentals; children's programs; concierge; car-rental desk; courtesy shopping shuttle; business center; room service; massage; laundry service; dry cleaning. *In room:* A/C, TV, dataport, minibar, hair dryer, iron, safe.

Hermosa Inn 🎖🎖 *Finds*   This luxurious boutique hotel, once a guest ranch, is now one of the few hotels in the Phoenix area to offer a bit of Old Arizona atmosphere. Originally built in 1930 as the home of cowboy artist Lon Megargee, the inn is situated in a quiet residential neighborhood on more than 6 acres of neatly landscaped gardens. If you don't like the crowds at big resorts but do enjoy the luxury at them, this is the spot for you. Rooms vary from cozy to spacious and are individually decorated in tastefully contemporary Western decor. The largest suites, which have more Southwestern flavor than just about any other rooms in the area, incorporate a mixture of contemporary and antique furnishings. The dining room, Lon's, is located in the original adobe home and serves excellent cuisine in a rustic, upscale setting (p. 82).

5532 N. Palo Cristi Rd., Paradise Valley, AZ 85253. © **800/241-1210** or 602/955-8614. Fax 602/955-8299. www.hermosainn.com. 35 units. Early Jan to Apr $285–$355 double, $475–$695 suite; early May to mid-May $220–$240 double, $360–$550 suite; late May to mid-Sept $95–$140 double, $300–$450 suite; late Sept to Dec $240–$290 double, $425–$625 suite. Rates include continental breakfast. AE, DC, DISC, MC, V. Take 32nd St. north from Camelback Rd., turn right on Stanford Rd., and turn left on N. Palo Cristi Rd. From Lincoln Dr., turn south on N. Palo Christi Rd. (east of 32nd St.). Pets under 20 lb. accepted ($250 deposit, $50 nonrefundable). **Amenities:** Restaurant (New American/Southwestern); lounge; outdoor pool; 2 Jacuzzis; 3 tennis courts; access to nearby health club; concierge; business center; room service; massage; laundry service; dry cleaning. *In room:* A/C, TV, dataport, minibar, hair dryer.

The Ritz-Carlton Phoenix 🏵🏵   Located across the street from the Biltmore Fashion Park shopping center in the heart of the Camelback Corridor business and shopping district, the Ritz-Carlton is the city's finest nonresort hotel and is known for its impeccable service. The public areas are filled with European antiques, and although this decor might seem a bit out of place in Phoenix, it's still utterly sophisticated. In the guest rooms, you'll find reproductions of antique furniture and marble bathrooms with ornate fixtures. An elegant lobby lounge serves afternoon tea as well as cocktails, while a clublike lounge offers fine cigars and premium spirits.

2401 E. Camelback Rd., Phoenix, AZ 85016. © **800/241-3333** or 602/468-0700. Fax 602/553-0685. 281 units. Oct–Apr $395–$455 double, $595–$2,500 suite; May $335–$395 double, $535–$2,500 suite; June–Aug $129–$355 double, $435–$2,500 suite; Sept $229–$395 double, $535–$2,500 suite. AE, DC, DISC, MC, V. Valet parking $22. **Amenities:** Restaurant (French bistro); 2 lounges; pool; health club; saunas; bike rentals; concierge; car-rental desk; business center; 24-hr. room service; massage; babysitting; laundry service; dry cleaning. *In room:* A/C, TV, dataport, minibar, hair dryer, iron, safe.

Royal Palms Hotel and Casitas 🏵🏵   Located midway between Old Town Scottsdale and Biltmore Fashion Park, the Royal Palms is one of the most romantic resorts in the valley. The main building, constructed more than 50 years ago, was built by Cunard Steamship executive Delos Cooke in the Spanish Mission style and is filled with European antiques that once belonged to Cooke. Surrounding the building, and giving the property the tranquil feel of a Mediterranean cloister, are lush walled gardens where antique fountains splash. The most memorable guest rooms are the deluxe casitas, each with a distinctive decor (ranging from opulent contemporary to classic European), private back patio, and front patio that can be enclosed by heavy curtains. The antiques-filled dining room, T. Cook's, is one of the city's most romantic restaurants (p. 82). An adjacent bar/lounge conjures up a Spanish villa setting

The new Alvadora Spa Royal Palms is scheduled to open in January 2003. This spa should make a stay at this utterly romantic resort just that much more hedonistic. Indoor/outdoor showers, a grotto waterfall shower, and spa therapy rooms with private gardens and fountains are just some of the anticipated features.

5200 E. Camelback Rd., Phoenix, AZ 85018. ℂ 800/672-6011 or 602/840-3610. Fax 602/840-6927. www.royalpalmshotel.com. 116 units. Jan–May $365–$385 double, $405–$3,500 suite; June to early Sept $169–$179 double, $189–$2,500 suite; mid-Sept to Dec $345–$365 double, $375–$3,500 suite (plus daily service fee of $18, year-round). AE, DC, DISC, MC, V. **Amenities:** Restaurant (Mediterranean); snack bar; lounge; outdoor pool with cabanas; tennis court; large exercise room; access to nearby health club; Jacuzzi; concierge; car-rental desk; business center; 24-hr. room service; massage; laundry service; dry cleaning. *In room:* A/C, TV, dataport, minibar, coffeemaker, hair dryer, iron, safe.

EXPENSIVE

Embassy Suites Biltmore ✦✦   Located across the parking lot from the Biltmore Fashion Park (Phoenix's most upscale shopping center), this hotel makes a great base if you want to be within walking distance of half a dozen good restaurants. The enormous atrium is filled with interesting tile work and other artistic Southwestern touches, as well as tropical greenery, waterfalls, and ponds filled with koi (colorful Japanese carp). The hotel's atrium also houses the breakfast area and a romantic lounge with huge banquettes shaded by palm trees. Unfortunately, the rooms, all suites, are dated and a bit of a letdown, but they're certainly large. All in all, this hotel is a good value, especially when you consider that rates include both breakfast and afternoon drinks.

2630 E. Camelback Rd., Phoenix, AZ 85016. ℂ 800/EMBASSY or 602/955-3992. Fax 602/955-6479. www.embassy-suites.com. 232 units. Jan to late Mar $209–$289 double; Apr to late May $159–$219 double; June to early Sept $109–$159 double; mid-Sept to Dec $179–$259 double. Rates include full breakfast and afternoon drinks. AE, DC, DISC, MC, V. Valet parking, $8. Pets accepted

($25). **Amenities:** Restaurant (steakhouse); lounge; large outdoor pool; Jacuzzi; exercise room; concierge; courtesy car; business center; room service; laundry service; coin-op laundry; dry cleaning. *In room:* A/C, TV, dataport, fridge, coffeemaker, microwave, hair dryer, iron.

MODERATE

Hacienda Alta *(Finds)* Located adjacent to the Phoenician, yet very much in its own separate world surrounded by a desert landscape, Hacienda Alta offers a convenient location, reasonable rates, and a chance to feel away from it all in the middle of the city. Don't expect the fussiness of most other B&Bs; owners Margaret and Ed Newhall make this casual, eclectic place a fun home away from home. The inn is a 1920s territorial-style adobe home, and in the old gardens are orange and grapefruit trees that often provide the juice for breakfast. Among the rooms, there's also a large suite with a sleeping loft, whirlpool tub, fireplace, and balcony overlooking the Phoenician's golf course.

5750 E. Camelback Rd., Phoenix, AZ 85018. © 480/945-8525. 3 units. $100–$125 double; $150 suite. Rates include full breakfast. No credit cards. **Amenities:** Access to nearby health club; concierge (fee); babysitting; laundry service. *In room:* A/C, TV, fridge, hair dryer, iron.

Maricopa Manor Centrally located between downtown Phoenix and Scottsdale, this bed-and-breakfast is just a block off busy Camelback Road, and for many years has been Phoenix's best official B&B. The inn's main building, designed to resemble a Spanish manor house, was built in 1928, and the orange trees, palms, and large yard all lend an Old Phoenix atmosphere. All guest rooms are large suites, and although some of the furnishings are a bit dated, several units have been recently renovated; for the most part, accommodations are quite comfortable. One suite has a sunroom and kitchen, while another has two separate sleeping areas. There are tables in the garden where you can eat your breakfast, which is delivered to your door.

15 W. Pasadena Ave., Phoenix, AZ 85013. © 800/292-6403 or 602/274-6302. Fax 602/266-3904. www.maricopamanor.com. 7 units. Sept–May $129–$219 double; June–Aug $99–$109 double. Rates include continental breakfast. AE, DC, DISC, MC, V. **Amenities:** Outdoor pool; access to nearby health club; Jacuzzi. *In room:* A/C, TV, dataport, fridge, coffeemaker, hair dryer, iron.

Sierra Suites Billing itself as a temporary residence and offering discounts for stays of 5 days or more, this hotel consists of studio-style apartments located just north of Camelback Road and not far from Biltmore Fashion Park. Although designed primarily for corporate business travelers on temporary assignment in the area,

(Kids) Family-Friendly Hotels

Doubletree La Posada Resort (p. 45) If you're a kid, it's hard to imagine a cooler pool than the one here. It's got a two-story waterfall, a swim-through cave, and big artificial boulders. There are also horseshoe pits, a volleyball court, and a pitch-and-putt green.

Holiday Inn SunSpree Resort (p. 47) Reasonable rates, a good Scottsdale location adjacent to the McCormick-Stillman Railroad Park, lots of grass for running around on, and free meals for kids under 12 make this one of the valley's best choices for families on a budget.

Hyatt Regency Scottsdale (p. 42) Not only is there a totally awesome water playground complete with sand beach and water slide, but the Kamp Hyatt Kachina program also provides supervised, structured activities.

The Phoenician (p. 43) Kids absolutely love the water slide here, and both parents and children appreciate the Funicians Club, a supervised activities program for those ages 5 to 12. A putting green and croquet court offer further diversions.

Pointe Hilton Squaw Peak Resort (p. 58) A water slide, a tubing river, a waterfall, water volleyball, miniature golf, a game room, and a children's program guarantee that your kids will be exhausted by the end of the day.

this lodging makes a good choice for families as well. All units have full kitchens, big closets and bathrooms, and separate sitting areas.

5235 N. 16th St., Phoenix, AZ 85016. © 800/4-SIERRA or 602/265-6800. Fax 602/265-1114. www.sierrasuites.com. 113 units. $69–$149 double. AE, DISC, MC, V. **Amenities:** Small outdoor pool; exercise room; Jacuzzi; coin-op laundry; dry cleaning. *In room:* A/C, TV, dataport, kitchen, coffeemaker, hair dryer, iron.

4 North Phoenix

Some of the valley's best scenery is to be found in north Phoenix, where several small mountains have been protected as parks and preserves; the two Pointe Hilton resorts claim great locations close to these parks. However, the valley's best shopping and dining, as well as most major attractions, are all at least a 30-minute drive away (through generally unattractive parts of the city).

VERY EXPENSIVE

Pointe Hilton Squaw Peak Resort 𝒜𝒜𝒜 (Kids)   Located at the foot of Squaw Peak, this lushly landscaped resort makes a big splash with its Hole-in-the-Wall River Ranch, a 9-acre aquatic playground that features a tubing "river," water slide, waterfall, sports pool, and lagoon pool. An 18-hole putting course and game room also help make it a great family vacation spot. The resort is done in the Spanish villa style, and most of the guest rooms are large suites outfitted with a mix of contemporary and Spanish colonial–style furnishings. The resort's Mexican restaurant is located in an 1880 adobe building, and there are enough other restaurants and snack bars to keep you content here for a long stay.

7677 N. 16th St., Phoenix, AZ 85020-9832. ⓒ **800/876-4683** or 602/997-2626. Fax 602/997-2391. www.pointehilton.com. 563 units. Jan to late Apr $199–$309 double, $950 grande suite; May and mid-Sept to Dec $109–$249 double, $659 grande suite; June to early Sept $109–$159 double, $659 grande suite (plus daily resort fee of $9, year-round). AE, DC, DISC, MC, V. **Amenities:** 3 restaurants (American/Southwestern, Mexican, steakhouse); 2 snack bars; 5 lounges; 7 pools; 18-hole golf course (4 miles away by shuttle); 4 tennis courts; health club and small spa; 6 Jacuzzis; saunas; bike rentals; children's programs; concierge; car-rental desk; business center; room service; massage; babysitting; laundry service; coin-op laundry; dry cleaning. *In room:* A/C, TV, dataport, minibar, coffeemaker, hair dryer, iron.

Pointe Hilton Tapatio Cliffs Resort 𝒜𝒜𝒜   If you love to lounge by the pool, then this resort is a great choice. The Falls, a 3-acre water playground, includes two lagoon pools, a 138-foot water slide, 40-foot cascades, a whirlpool tucked into an artificial grotto, and rental cabanas for that extra dash of luxury. Hikers will enjoy the easy access to trails in the adjacent North Mountain Recreation Area, while golfers can avail themselves of the resort's course. All rooms are spacious suites with Southwest-inspired furnishings; corner units are particularly bright. Situated on the shoulder of North Mountain, this resort has steep roads and walkways (get your heart and brakes checked); at the top of the property is Different Pointe of View, a pricey restaurant with one of the finest views in the city (p. 90).

11111 N. Seventh St., Phoenix, AZ 85020. ⓒ **800/876-4683** or 602/866-7500. Fax 602/993-0276. www.pointehilton.com. 585 units. Jan to late Apr $199–$299 double, $899 grande suite; May and mid-Sept to Dec $109–$249 double, $749 grande suite; June to early Sept $109–$159 double, $559 grande suite (plus daily resort fee of $9, year-round). AE, DC, DISC, MC, V. **Amenities:** 3 restaurants (French, American, steakhouse); 2 poolside cafes; 4 lounges; 7 pools; golf course; 12 tennis courts; fitness center; small full-service spa; 8 Jacuzzis; sauna; steam room; bike rentals; horseback riding; children's programs; concierge; car-rental desk; free shuttle between Pointe Hilton properties; business center; pro shop; room service; massage; babysitting; laundry service; dry cleaning. *In room:* A/C, TV, dataport, minibar, coffeemaker, hair dryer, iron.

EXPENSIVE

Embassy Suites–Phoenix North ★★ (Value) This resortlike hotel in north Phoenix is right off I-17, a 30- to 45-minute drive from the rest of the valley's resorts (and good restaurants)—but if you happen to have relatives in Sun City or are planning a trip north to Sedona or the Grand Canyon, it's a good choice. The lobby of the Mission-style hotel has the feel of a Spanish church interior, but instead of a cloister off the lobby, there's a garden courtyard with a huge pool and lots of palm trees. The guest rooms are all suites, although furnishings are fairly basic and bathrooms small.

2577 W. Greenway Rd., Phoenix, AZ 85023. © **800/EMBASSY** or 602/375-1777. Fax 602/993-5963. www.embassy-suites.com. 314 units. $79–$169 double. Rates include full breakfast. AE, DC, DISC, MC, V. **Amenities:** Restaurant; lounge; snack bar; complimentary cocktail reception; large pool and children's pool; 2 tennis courts; volleyball court; exercise room; Jacuzzi; sauna; car-rental desk; room service; laundry service; coin-op laundry; dry cleaning. *In room:* A/C, TV, dataport, fridge, coffeemaker, iron.

MODERATE/INEXPENSIVE

Among the better moderately priced chain motels in north Phoenix are the **Best Western Inn Suites Hotel Phoenix,** 1615 E. Northern Ave., at 16th Street (© **800/752-2204** or 602/997-6285), charging high-season rates of $119 to $159 double; and the **Best Western Bell Hotel,** 17211 N. Black Canyon Hwy. (© **877/263-1290** or 602/993-8300), charging $89 to $119 double.

Among the better budget chain motels are the **Motel 6–Sweetwater,** 2735 W. Sweetwater Ave. (© **800/4-MOTEL-6** or 602/942-5030), charging $46 to $54 double; and **Super 8–Phoenix Metro/Central,** 4021 N. 27th Ave. (© **800/800-8000** or 602/248-8880), with doubles for $50 to $56.

5 Downtown Phoenix

Unless you're a sports fan or are in town for a convention, there's not much to recommend in downtown Phoenix. You can walk to the Bank One Ballpark and America West Arena, but this 9-to-5 area can feel like a modern ghost town.

VERY EXPENSIVE

Crowne Plaza–Phoenix Downtown ★ This 19-story business and convention hotel is one of the best choices in downtown, although with the crowds of conventioneers, individual travelers may feel overlooked. A Mediterranean villa theme has been adopted throughout the public areas, with slate flooring and walls painted to resemble cracked stucco. Guest rooms, all of which were renovated in 2001, are designed with the business traveler in mind.

100 N. First St., Phoenix, AZ 85004. ✆ **800/2-CROWNE** or 602/333-0000. Fax 602/333-5181. www.phxcp.com. 532 units. Late Sept to mid-May $250–$290 double, $300–$1,300 suite; late May to mid-Sept $150–$190 double, $200–$900 suite. AE, DC, DISC, MC, V. Valet parking $10. **Amenities:** Restaurant (American); 2 cafes; comedy club; outdoor pool; exercise room; access to nearby health club; sauna; concierge; business center; salon; room service; laundry service; dry cleaning. *In room:* A/C, TV, dataport, coffeemaker, hair dryer, iron.

EXPENSIVE

Hyatt Regency Phoenix 𝒦𝒦   Located directly across the street from the Phoenix Civic Plaza, this high-rise Hyatt is almost always packed with conventioneers. Whether full or empty, the hotel seems somewhat understaffed, so don't expect top-notch service. Guest rooms are fairly standard, though comfortably furnished. Ask for one above the eighth floor to take advantage of the views from the glass elevators. The rotating rooftop restaurant is one of the best reasons to stay at this big convention hotel.

122 N. Second St., Phoenix, AZ 85004. ✆ **800/233-1234** or 602/252-1234. Fax 602/256-0801. www.phoenix.hyatt.com. 712 units. $125–$290 double, from $500 suite. AE, DC, DISC, MC, V. Valet parking $18; self-parking $14. **Amenities:** 3 restaurants (Southwestern, American); 2 lounges; small outdoor pool; exercise room; access to nearby health club; Jacuzzi; concierge; car-rental desk; business center; shopping arcade; room service; babysitting; laundry service; dry cleaning. *In room:* A/C, TV, dataport, coffeemaker, hair dryer.

MODERATE

Hotel San Carlos 𝒦   If you don't mind staying in downtown Phoenix with the convention crowds, you'll get good value at this historic hotel. Built in 1928 and listed on the National Register of Historic Places, the San Carlos provides that touch of elegance and charm missing from the other downtown choices. Unfortunately, bedrooms are rather small by today's standards, and the decor needs updating.

202 N. Central Ave., Phoenix, AZ 85004. ✆ **602/253-4121**. Fax 602/253-4121. www.hotelsancarlos.com. 133 units. Jan–Apr $149 double, $210 suite; May–Sept $99 double, $149 suite; Oct–Dec $125 double, $199 suite. Rates include continental breakfast. AE, DC, DISC, MC, V. Valet and self-parking $15. Pets allowed ($25). **Amenities:** 2 restaurants (Irish pub, espresso bar); rooftop pool; concierge; laundry service; dry cleaning. *In room:* A/C, TV, dataport, coffeemaker, iron.

6 Tempe, Mesa, South Phoenix & the Airport Area

For the most part, south Phoenix is one of the poorest parts of the city. However, it does have a couple of exceptional resorts, and Phoenix South Mountain Park is one of the best places in the city to experience the desert. Tempe, which lies just a few miles east of the airport, is home to Arizona State University, and consequently supports a lively nightlife scene. Along Tempe's Mill Avenue, you'll find one of the only neighborhoods in the valley where locals actually get out of their cars and walk the streets. Tempe is also convenient to Papago Park, which is home to the Phoenix Zoo, the Desert Botanical Garden, the Arizona Historical Society Museum, a municipal golf course, and hiking and mountain-biking trails.

VERY EXPENSIVE

The Buttes, A Wyndham Resort ★★   This spectacular resort, only 3 miles from Sky Harbor Airport, makes the most of its craggy hilltop location. Although some people complain that the freeway in the foreground ruins the view, the rocky setting and desert landscaping leave no doubt you're in the Southwest. From the cactus garden, stream, waterfall, and fishpond *inside* the lobby to the circular restaurant and free-form swimming pools, every inch of this resort is calculated to take your breath away. The pools (complete with waterfalls) and four whirlpools (one of which is the most romantic in the valley) are the best reasons to stay here. Guest rooms are stylishly elegant. The valley/highway-view rooms are a bit larger than the pool-view rooms, but second-floor pool-view rooms have patios. Unfortunately for fans of long soaks, most bathrooms have only three-quarter-size tubs. The Top of the Rock restaurant snags the best view around, and sunset dinners are memorable (p. 90).

2000 Westcourt Way, Tempe, AZ 85282. (© **800/WYNDHAM** or 602/225-9000. Fax 602/438-8622. www.wyndham.com. 353 units. Jan–Apr $239–$289 double, $475–$575 suite; May and mid-Sept to Dec $139–$189 double, from $475 suite; June to early Sept $109–$169 double, from $375 suite. AE, DC, DISC, MC, V. **Amenities:** 2 restaurants (New American/Southwestern, American); 3 lounges; snack bar; 2 pools; 4 tennis courts; volleyball courts; exercise room; access to nearby health club; spa services; 4 Jacuzzis; sauna; concierge; business center; room service; massage; dry cleaning. *In room:* A/C, TV, dataport, coffeemaker, hair dryer, iron.

Pointe South Mountain Resort ★★★ *(Kids)*   Located on the south side of the valley, this sprawling resort abuts the 17,000-acre South Mountain Park, and although the property's grand scale seems designed primarily to accommodate convention crowds, individual travelers will likely benefit from the great location and find plenty to keep themselves busy. Golfers get great views from the greens, while urban cowboys can ride right into the sunset on South Mountain. With the addition in 2002 of the new Oasis water park (complete with a wave pool and water slides), this has become one of the valley's premier family resorts. The guest rooms, all suites, feature contemporary Southwestern furnishings. Mountainside units offer the best views of the golf course and South Mountain. There's a wide range of restaurant choices, including Rustler's Rooste, a cowboy steakhouse that serves rattlesnake appetizers (p. 91).

7777 S. Pointe Pkwy., Phoenix, AZ 85044. ℂ **877/800-4888** or 602/438-9000. Fax 602/431-6425. www.pointesouthmtn.com. 640 units. Mid-Sept to Apr $275–$325 double, from $475 suite; May $235–$285 double, from $435 suite; June to early Sept $155–$205 double, from $355 suite (plus daily resort fee of $10, year-round). AE, DC, DISC, MC, V. **Amenities:** 4 restaurants (Continental, steakhouse, Mexican, Southwestern); 2 snack bars; 3 lounges; 8 outdoor pools; 18-hole golf course; 8 tennis courts; volleyball courts; racquetball court; pro shop; health club; full-service spa; 3 Jacuzzis; children's programs; horseback riding; concierge; car-rental desk; business center; room service; massage; babysitting; laundry service; coin-op laundry; dry cleaning. *In room:* A/C, TV, dataport, minibar, coffeemaker, hair dryer, iron.

EXPENSIVE

Fiesta Inn Resort ⓖ *Value*   Reasonable rates, green lawns, palm- and eucalyptus-shaded grounds, extensive recreational facilities, and a location close to the airport, ASU, and Tempe's Mill Avenue make this older, casual resort one of the best deals in the valley. Okay, so it isn't as fancy as the resorts in Scottsdale, but you can't argue with the rates. The large guest rooms were all renovated in 2000, and though a bit dark, they have an appealing retro Mission styling. You may not feel like you're in the desert when you stay here (due to the lawns and shade trees), but you'll certainly get a lot more for your money than at other area hotels in this price range.

2100 S. Priest Dr., Tempe, AZ 85282. ℂ **800/528-6481** or 480/967-1441. Fax 480/967-0224. www.fiestainnresort.com. 270 units. Jan to mid-Apr $175 double; late Apr to May $140 double; June–Sept $89 double; Oct–Dec $165 double. AE, DC, DISC, MC, V. Pets accepted. **Amenities:** Restaurant (American/Southwestern); lounge; pool; putting green and driving range; 3 tennis courts; exercise room; Jacuzzi; bike rentals; concierge; car-rental desk; courtesy airport shuttle; business center; room service; babysitting; laundry service; dry cleaning. *In room:* A/C, TV, dataport, fridge, coffeemaker, hair dryer, iron.

Tempe Mission Palms Hotel ⓖ   College students, their families, and anyone else who wants to be close to Tempe's nightlife will find this an ideal, although somewhat overpriced, location right in the heart of the Mill Avenue shopping, restaurant, and nightlife district. When you've had enough of the hustle and bustle, you can retreat to the hotel's rooftop pool. For the most part, guest rooms are quite comfortable and boast lots of wood, marble, and granite.

60 E. Fifth St., Tempe, AZ 85281. ℂ 800/547-8705 or 480/894-1400. Fax 480/968-7677. www.missionpalms.com. 303 units. Sept–Mar $149–$199 double, from $399 suite; Apr–May $119–$169 double, from $299 suite; June–Aug $79–$99 double, from $199 suite. AE, DC, DISC, MC, V. Pets accepted ($100 deposit, $25 non-refundable). **Amenities:** Restaurant (Southwestern); 2 lounges; medium-size outdoor pool; tennis court; exercise room; access to nearby health club; 2 Jacuzzis; concierge; courtesy airport shuttle; business center; room service; laundry service; dry cleaning. *In room:* A/C, TV, dataport, coffeemaker, hair dryer, iron.

Twin Palms Hotel ⓐ   Although the rooms at this mid-rise hotel, located right off the ASU campus, are just standard, the Twin Palms is a great choice for fitness fanatics. Guests have full access to the nearby ASU Student Recreation Complex, which includes a huge weight-training room; Olympic-size pool; and racquetball, tennis, and basketball courts. The hotel is also close to Sun Devil Stadium, the ASU-Karsten Golf Course, and busy Mill Avenue.

225 E. Apache Blvd., Tempe, AZ 85281. ℂ 800/367-0835 or 480/967-9431. Fax 480/303-6602. www.twinpalmshotel.com. 139 units. Jan–Apr $159–$189 double; May–Sept $59–$79 double; Oct–Dec $129–$159 double. AE, DC, DISC, MC, V. **Amenities:** Lounge; outdoor pool; access to nearby gym; concierge; car-rental desk; courtesy airport shuttle; 24-hr. room service; coin-op laundry; dry cleaning. *In room:* A/C, TV, dataport, coffeemaker, hair dryer, iron.

MODERATE/INEXPENSIVE

Apache Boulevard in Tempe becomes Main Street in Mesa, and along this stretch of road there are numerous old motels charging some of the lowest rates in the valley. However, these motels are very hit-or-miss. If you're used to staying at non-chain motels, you might want to cruise this strip and check out a few places. Otherwise, try the chain motels mentioned below (which tend to charge $20–$40 more per night than non-chain motels).

Chain options in the Tempe area include the **Days Inn–Tempe,** 1221 E. Apache Blvd. (ℂ 480/968-7793), charging $50 to $119 double; and **Super 8–Tempe/Scottsdale,** 1020 E. Apache Blvd. (ℂ 480/967-8891), charging $70 to $100 double.

Chain options in the Mesa area include the **Days Inn–Mesa,** 333 W. Juanita Ave. (ℂ 480/844-8900), charging $49 to $99 double; **Motel 6–Mesa,** 336 W. Hampton Ave. (ℂ 480/844-8899), charging $52 to $56 double; and **Super 8–Mesa,** 6733 E. Main St. (ℂ 480/981-6181), charging $62 to $84 double.

Chain options in the airport area include the **Best Western Airport Inn,** 2425 S. 24th St. (© **602/273-7251**), charging $79 to $130 double; and **Rodeway Inn–Airport East,** 1550 S. 52nd St. (© **480/967-3000**), charging $90 to $110 double. All rates are for high season.

7 Outlying Resorts

Gold Canyon Golf Resort ★★ *Value*   Located way out on the east side of the valley near Apache Junction (at least a 30- to 45-min. drive from the airport), Gold Canyon is a favorite of devoted golfers who come to play some of the most scenic holes in the state (the Superstition Mountains provide the backdrop). Although non-golfers will appreciate the scenery, the small pool and the lack of an exercise room make it clear that golfers, not swimmers, take the fore here. The spacious guest rooms are housed in blindingly white pueblo-inspired buildings; some have fireplaces, while others have whirlpools. Be sure to opt for a deluxe golf-course room. The limited dining options here and in the immediate vicinity are a drawback, but if golf is your game and you've just got to play the Dinosaur Mountain course, then the lack of menu variety shouldn't matter too much.

6100 S. Kings Ranch Rd., Gold Canyon, AZ 85218. © **800/624-6445** or 480/982-9090. Fax 480/983-9554. www.gcgr.com. 101 units. Mid-Jan to mid-Apr $235–$310 double; late Apr to mid-Sept $135–$210 double; late Sept to early Jan $185–$260 double. AE, DC, DISC, MC, V. Pets accepted ($50). **Amenities:** 2 restaurants (American); lounge; pool; 2 highly regarded 18-hole golf courses; small spa; Jacuzzi; bike rentals; horseback riding; concierge; room service; babysitting; laundry service; dry cleaning. *In room:* A/C, TV, dataport, fridge, coffeemaker, hair dryer, iron.

The Wigwam Resort ★★   Located 20 minutes west of downtown Phoenix and more than twice as far from Scottsdale, this property opened its doors to the public in 1929 and remains one of the nation's premier golf resorts. Three challenging golf courses and superb service are the reasons most people choose this resort, which, although elegant, is set amid flatland that lacks the stunning desert scenery of the Scottsdale area. The Wigwam has a very traditional feel about it, right down to the skeet and trap shooting range. Most of the guest rooms are in Santa Fe–style buildings, surrounded by green lawns and colorful gardens, and all of the spacious units feature contemporary Southwestern furniture. Some units have fireplaces, but the rooms to request are those along the golf course.

300 Wigwam Blvd., Litchfield Park, AZ 85340. (✆) **800/327-0396** or 623/935-3811. Fax 623/935-3737. www.wigwamresort.com. 331 units. Early Jan to mid-May $369 double, from $429 suite; late May to early Sept $185 double, from $225 suite; mid-Sept to Dec $285 double, from $310 suite (plus daily resort fee of $12, year-round). AE, DC, DISC, MC, V. Pets under 20 lb. accepted ($50 deposit, $25 nonrefundable). **Amenities:** 3 restaurants (Continental, Southwestern, American); 2 lounges; afternoon tea; snack bar; 2 pools; 3 18-hole golf courses; putting green; 9 tennis courts; volleyball court; croquet court; exercise room; spa services; Jacuzzi; sauna; bike rentals; children's programs; concierge; activities desk; car-rental desk; golf and tennis pro shops; 24-hr. room service; massage; babysitting; laundry service; dry cleaning. *In room:* A/C, TV, dataport, minibar, coffeemaker, hair dryer, iron, safe.

5

Where to Dine

The Valley of the Sun boasts some excellent restaurants, with most of the best dining options concentrated in the Scottsdale Road and Biltmore Corridor areas. If you want to splurge on only one expensive meal while you're here, consider a resort restaurant that offers a view of the city lights. Other meals not to be missed are the cowboy dinners served amid Wild West decor at such places as Pinnacle Peak and Rustler's Rooste.

Phoenix also has plenty of big and familiar chains. At the **Hard Rock Cafe,** 2621 E. Camelback Rd. (© **602/956-3669**), you can toss down a burger and buy that all-important T-shirt to prove you were here. There's a **California Pizza Kitchen,** 2400 E. Camelback Rd. (© **602/553-8382**), in Phoenix's Biltmore Fashion Park, and another branch in Scottsdale at 10100 Scottsdale Rd., 1 block south of Shea Boulevard (© **480/596-8300**).

The big chain steakhouses are also duking it out here. You'll find two **Ruth's Chris** steakhouses: in the Biltmore district, 2201 E. Camelback Rd. (© **602/957-9600**), and in the Scottsdale Seville shopping plaza, 7001 N. Scottsdale Rd. (© **480/991-5988**). **Morton's Steakhouses** are located in the Biltmore district in the Shops at the Esplanade, 2501 E. Camelback Rd. (© **602/ 955-9577**), and in north Scottsdale, 15233 N. Kierland Blvd. (© **480/951-4440**).

Good places to go trolling for a place to eat include the trendy Biltmore Fashion Park and Old Town Scottsdale. At the former, which by the way is a shopping mall, not a park, you'll find the chain restaurant California Pizza Kitchen (mentioned above) as well as nearly a dozen other excellent restaurants. In downtown Scottsdale, within an area of roughly 4 square blocks, you'll find about a dozen good restaurants.

If you happen to be visiting the Phoenix Art Museum, the Heard Museum, or the Desert Botanical Garden anytime around lunch, stay put for your noon meal. All three attractions have cafes serving decent, if limited, menus.

See the end of this chapter for information restaurants with a view, "cowboy steakhouses", breakfast and brunch spots, and cafes.

1 Scottsdale

EXPENSIVE

Bloom *⋪⋪* *Value* NEW AMERICAN   Located in the upscale Shops at Gainey Village, Bloom is big and always full of energy. The minimalist decor emphasizes flowers, an elegant wine bar serves a wide range of flights (tasting assortments), and the bistro-style menu has lots of great dishes in a wide range of prices. Opt for one of the salads, such as fresh artichoke hearts with shaved Parmesan and white-truffle drizzle; there are also enough interesting appetizers that a dinner of small plates would be extremely satisfying. Among the entrees, the roast duck with a crisp potato nest and drunken cherry sauce is excellent. Whatever you do, do not miss the Bars of Sin dessert!

8877 N. Scottsdale Rd. *℃* **480/922-5666.** www.tasteofbloom.com. Reservations recommended. Main courses $7–$12 lunch, $12–$24 dinner. AE, MC, V. Mon–Thurs 11am–2:30pm and 5–9:30pm; Fri–Sat 11am–2:30pm and 5–10:30pm.

Cowboy Ciao Wine Bar & Grill *⋪* SOUTHWESTERN/ FUSION   Delicious food and a fun, trendy atmosphere outfitted in "cowboy chic" make this a great place for a memorable meal. Located in fashionable downtown Scottsdale, it attracts a diverse group of people. The not-to-be-missed dishes are the exotic mushroom pan-fry and the TM soup. The porcini-crusted rib-eye steak is another good choice for mushroom fans. Cowboy Ciao is also notable for its wine list and bar, where customers can order a flight (tasting) of wines. If you're feeling adventurous when it comes time for dessert, opt for the Mexican chocolate pot de crème with chipotle pepper cream. Unfortunately, service here can be uneven.

7133 E. Stetson Dr. (at Sixth Ave.). *℃* **480/WINE-111.** www.cowboyciao.com. Reservations recommended. Main courses $7–$22 lunch, $17–$32 dinner. AE, DC, DISC, MC, V. Tues–Sat 11:30am–2:30pm and 5–10pm; Sun–Mon 5–10pm.

El Chorro Lodge *⋪* CONTINENTAL   Built in 1934 as a school for girls and converted to a lodge and restaurant 3 years later, El Chorro is a valley landmark and one of the area's last old traditional establishments. Even if the interior is a little dowdy, at nighttime the lights twinkle on the saguaro cactus and the restaurant takes on a timeless tranquillity. The adobe building houses several dining rooms, but the patio is the place to be, either in the daytime or on

Phoenix, Scottsdale & the Valley of the Sun Dining

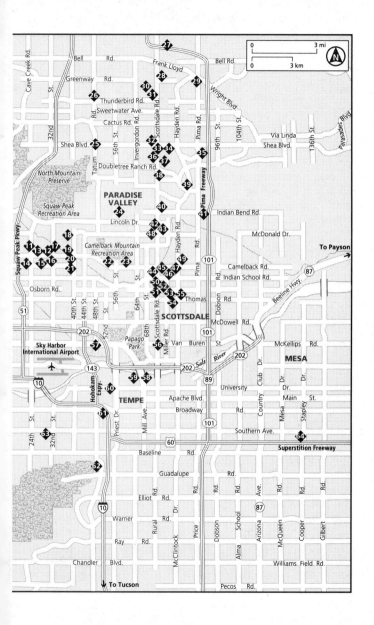

a chilly night, when there's a fire crackling in the patio fireplace. Both old-timers and families like the traditional decor and menu, which features such classics as chateaubriand and rack of lamb. In addition to the favorites, there are several low-fat and low-salt dishes, as well as seafood options. Save room for the legendary sticky buns.

5550 E. Lincoln Dr. ✆ 480/948-5170. Reservations recommended. Main courses $9–$17 lunch, $15–$30 dinner. AE, DC, DISC, MC, V. Mon–Fri 11am–3pm and 5:30–11pm; Sat 5:30–11pm; Sun 10am–2pm and 5:30–11pm.

Golden Swan ✸✸✸ SOUTHWESTERN   If you're looking for distinctive Southwestern flavors in an unforgettable setting, this is the place. Golden Swan is located at the Hyatt Regency Scottsdale, which, with its royal palms, geometric architecture, and fountains, is one of the valley's most beautiful resorts. The menu has plenty of bold flavors. Start your meal with crab cakes with pine nuts and jicama-papaya slaw. Entrees such as the grilled shrimp and scallops with a *huitlacoche* quesadilla are always artistically arranged. (*Huitlacoche* is a type of mushroom popular in Mexico but rarely seen north of the border.) Be sure to request a seat on the sunken patio, which really is below water level (a wall keeps the water at bay). Before or after dinner, the resort's open-air lounge is a romantic spot for a drink.

At the Hyatt Regency Scottsdale, 7500 E. Doubletree Ranch Rd. ✆ **480/991-3388.** Reservations recommended. Main courses $28–$36; Sun brunch $42. AE, DC, DISC, MC, V. Daily 6–10pm; Sun brunch 10am–2pm.

Mancuso's ✸✸ NORTHERN ITALIAN/CONTINENTAL   With its ramparts, towers, stone walls, and narrow alleyways, the Borgata shopping plaza is modeled after the Tuscan village of San Gimignano, so it seems only fitting that Mancuso's would affect the look of an Italian castle banquet hall. A cathedral ceiling, arched windows, and huge roof beams set the stage for the gourmet cuisine; a pianist playing soft jazz sets the mood. If you lack the means to start your meal with the beluga caviar, perhaps *carpaccio di manzo*— sliced raw beef with mustard sauce and capers—will do. Veal is a specialty (with osso buco a long-time favorite), but it's always difficult just to get past the pasta offerings. Fish and daily seafood specials round out the menu. The professional service will have you feeling like royalty by the time you finish your dessert. Who needs a trip to Tuscany when you have Mancuso's?

At the Borgata, 6166 N. Scottsdale Rd. ✆ **480/948-9988.** Reservations recommended. Main courses $19–$30; pastas $17.50–$25. AE, DC, DISC, MC, V. Year-round daily 5–10pm; Oct to late Apr also open Mon–Fri 11:30am–2:30pm.

Medizona ⭐⭐ MEDITERRANEAN/SOUTHWESTERN
Foodies, take note: This downtown Scottsdale restaurant, though tucked away on an otherwise unremarkable street, is one of the most talked about establishments in town these days. Chef Lenard Rubin has worked his way through the area's top resort restaurants, including Windows on the Green at the Phoenician and the Palo Verde Room at the Boulders. As the restaurant's name implies, the menu here is a masterful blend of both the bold flavors of the Southwest and the more subtle flavors of the Mediterranean. Although it sounds a bit odd, the rabbit, fig, and pine-nut baklava is an excellent way to start a meal before moving on to achiote-rubbed salmon with crawfish-corn risotto. For dessert, how can you resist prickly-pear tiramisu with Turkish coffee–pistachio sauce? Just as we went to press, we found out that Medizona is under new ownership. Hopefully, the food will stay as eclectic and delicious as ever.

7217 E. Fourth Ave. © **480/947-9500.** Reservations highly recommended. Main courses $21–$29. AE, DC, MC, V. Tues–Sat 6–10pm.

Pepin ⭐ SPANISH For traditional Spanish fare and plenty of lively entertainment, you won't do better than Pepin. Located on the Scottsdale Mall, this small restaurant offers such a wide selection of tapas that you can easily have dinner without ever glancing at the main-course list. There are also several styles of paella, most of which are seafood extravaganzas. Thursday through Saturday evenings bring live flamenco performances, along with salsa dancing on Friday and Saturday. If you don't mind eating early, $15 four-course dinner specials are offered daily between 4:30 and 6:30pm.

7363 Scottsdale Mall. © **480/990-9026.** Reservations recommended. Main courses $16–$29; tapas $6–$11. AE, DC, DISC, MC, V. Tues–Thurs and Sun 4:30–10pm; Fri–Sat 11:30am–3pm and 4:30–11pm. Happy hour Tues–Fri 4:30–6:30pm.

Rancho Pinot ⭐⭐ NEW AMERICAN Rancho Pinot, hidden at the back of a nondescript shopping center adjacent to the upscale Borgata shopping plaza, combines a homey cowboy-chic decor with nonthreatening contemporary American cuisine, and has long been a favorite with Scottsdale and Phoenix residents. Look elsewhere if you're craving wildly creative flavor combinations, but if you like simple, well-prepared food, Rancho Pinot may be the place for you. Our favorite starter is the grilled squid salad with preserved lemon; for an entree, you can always count on the handmade pasta or Nonni's chicken, braised with white wine, mushrooms, and herbs. There's a short but well-chosen list of beers and wines by the glass.

The staff is friendly and treats you as though you're a regular, even if it's your first visit.

6208 N. Scottsdale Rd. (southwest corner of Scottsdale Rd. and Lincoln Dr.). ℭ 480/367-8030. Reservations recommended. Main courses $17.50–$29. AE, DISC, MC, V. Tues–Sat 5–10pm. Summer hours subject to change.

Restaurant Hapa 🅰🅰 PAN-ASIAN Even this far from the Pacific, pan-Asian cuisine can cause a stir, and if you've got deep pockets and a taste for unusual fusion fare, don't leave town without scheduling a meal here. Before your appetizer even arrives, you might snack on herb flatbread with a soy dipping sauce or a complimentary bite of coconut curry with pine nuts. We're particularly partial to the strong flavor combinations that can be found on the appetizer list: mussels in Thai coconut broth, charred beef salad, and fiery scallops with mango, lychee, and watercress. If the miso-marinated sea bass is on the menu, don't pass it up; on a recent visit, it proved to be the best piece of fish we'd ever tasted. The atmosphere is casual yet sophisticated, and attracts a lot of restaurant industry folks from around the valley.

6204 N. Scottsdale Rd. (southwest corner of Scottsdale Rd. and Lincoln Dr.). ℭ 480/998-8220. www.restauranthapa.com. Reservations recommended. Main courses $18–$34; tasting menu $60. AE, DC, MC, V. Mon–Sat 5:30–10pm.

Roaring Fork 🅰🅰 SOUTHWESTERN This trendy restaurant is the creation of chef Robert McGrath, who was once the chef at the Phoenician's Windows on the Green. At press time, Roaring Fork was in the process of moving to its new location in a corporate office building at the corner of North Scottsdale Road and Goldwater Boulevard. The food here is among the most creative Southwestern fare you'll find in the valley. The bread basket alone, filled with herb-infused rolls and corn muffins accompanied by honey-chile butter, is enough to make you weep with joy. Be sure you try the sugar-and-chile-cured duck breast with green-chile macaroni, a house specialty. If you can't get a table, dine at the bar, where you'll see bowls of interesting munchies such as spicy jerky. Don't miss the huckleberry margaritas.

N. Scottsdale Rd. at Goldwater Blvd. (north of Old Town). ℭ 480/947-0795. www.roaringfork.com. Reservations highly recommended. Main courses $17–$29. AE, DISC, MC, V. Mon–Sat 5:30–10pm.

Roy's of Scottsdale 🅰🅰 Value EURO-ASIAN So you decided to go to Arizona instead of Hawaii this year, but you really prefer Asian flavors to those of the Southwest. Don't worry—even in Scottsdale you can now get Hawaiian chef Roy Yamaguchi's terrific pan-Asian cuisine. Brilliant combinations and flamboyant presentations are the hallmarks, and despite the lively atmosphere, service usually runs like clockwork. The menu includes nightly specials such as caramelized onion and grilled chicken pizza, as well as such signature dishes as blackened ahi tuna with a soy-mustard butter sauce. If you can't get a reservation, try for a seat at the counter, which provides a great floor show of cooks preparing food at lightning speed.

There's another Roy's at 2501 E. Camelback Rd., in the Camelback Esplanade (© **602/381-1155**).

At the Scottsdale Seville shopping center, 7001 N. Scottsdale Rd. © **480/905-1155**. Reservations recommended. Main courses $17–$32; smaller plates $7.25–$11.50. AE, MC, V. Sun–Thurs 5–10pm; Fri–Sat 5–11pm.

MODERATE

Sam's Cafe, North Scottsdale Road and Shea Boulevard (© **480/368-2800**), which has other branches around the valley, is another area restaurant worth trying. For more information, see the review on p. 86.

Arcadia Farms ⭑ NEW AMERICAN   Long a favorite of the Scottsdale ladies-who-lunch crowd, this Old Town restaurant features a romantic setting and well-prepared contemporary fare. Arcadia Farms is committed to healthy food and sustainable agricultural practices, and only organic lettuces and herbs are used in the dishes served here. Try the raspberry goat cheese salad with jicama and candied pecans—it's delicious. The warm mushroom, spinach, and goat cheese tart is another winner. The patio, with its shade trees and mature plantings, is the preferred place to dine.

7014 E. First Ave. © **480/941-5665**. Reservations recommended. Main courses $10–$13. MC, V. Daily 11am–3pm.

Bandera ⭑ *Value* AMERICAN   Once you've gotten a whiff of the wood-roasted chickens turning on the rotisseries in Bandera's back-of-the-building, open-air stone oven, you'll know exactly what to order when you finally get seated at this perennially popular spot in Old Town. What an aroma! The succulent spit-roasted chicken is served with the ultimate comfort food, a mountain of creamy mashed potatoes flecked with green onion and black pepper. Sure, you could order prime rib or clams, but you'd be a fool if you did. Stick with the chicken or maybe the honey-barbecued ribs, and you won't go wrong. The succulent smoked-salmon appetizer is also a hit.

3821 N. Scottsdale Rd. © **480/994-3524**. Reservations not accepted. Main courses $9–$24. AE, DISC, MC, V. Sun–Thurs 4:30–10pm; Fri–Sat 4:30–11pm.

Carlsbad Tavern ⒜ NEW MEXICAN   Carlsbad Tavern blends the fiery tastes of New Mexican cuisine with a hip and humorous bat-theme atmosphere (a reference to Carlsbad Caverns). The menu lists traditional New Mexican dishes such as *carne adobada*, pork simmered in a fiery red-chile sauce, as well as nouvelle Southwestern specialties like grilled chicken, andouille sausage, and pine nuts tossed with pasta in a spicy peppercorn cream sauce. Cool off your taste buds with a margarita made with fresh-squeezed juice. A lagoon makes this place feel like a beach bar, while the patio fireplace is cozy on a cold night.

3313 N. Hayden Rd. (south of Osborn). ⒞ 480/970-8164. Reservations recommended for dinner. Main courses $6.25–$19. AE, DC, DISC, MC, V. Mon–Sat 11am–1am; Sun 1pm–1am (limited menu daily 10 or 11pm–1am).

L'Ecole ⒜ *Value* FRENCH/MEDITERANNEAN   This culinary opportunity is a well-kept local secret—there aren't many places where you can get a three-course lunch for $12 or a five-course dinner for $25. Although you don't have to bring a lot of money here, you do have to have a lot of patience—the cooking and serving is done by students from the Scottsdale Culinary Institute, and it's all a learning experience for them. The menu changes frequently, but you can expect a good mix of classic and contemporary dishes. There's a respectable selection of wines and liquors to accompany the meal.

The Scottsdale Culinary Institute also operates **L'Academie,** a more casual restaurant, at its satellite campus in the Scottsdale Galleria, 4301 N. Scottsdale Rd., near Old Town Scottsdale.

At the Scottsdale Culinary Institute, 8100 E. Camelback Rd. (just east of Hayden Rd.). ⒞ 480/990-3773. www.scichefs.com. Reservations highly recommended several days in advance. 3-course lunch $12–$14; 5-course dinner $25–$30. AE, DISC, MC, V. Mon–Fri 11am–12:15pm and 6–7:30pm. Closed every 3rd Mon.

6th Avenue Bistrot ⒜ CLASSIC FRENCH   Who says French has to be fussy? This little bistro less than a block off Scottsdale Road is, at lunch during the high season, as casual as a French restaurant gets (although it's a bit more formal in the evening). The draw here is a simple menu of reliable dishes at fairly reasonable prices. Get a bit of country paté, some tenderloin of pork with port-wine sauce, a hearty Beaujolais, top it off with *mousse au chocolat,* and *voilà*—you have a perfect French dinner. Lunch, in the months that it is served, is a great deal, and wines by the glass are reasonably priced.

7150 E. Sixth Ave. ⒞ 480/947-6022. Reservations recommended. Main courses $19–$23 dinner. AE, MC, V. Year-round Mon–Thurs 5–9pm, Fri–Sat 5–10pm; Nov–Apr also open Tues–Fri 11am–2pm.

Sushi Ko 🛫 *Finds* JAPANESE   Recommended by those who know good sushi and popular with the Japanese community, Sushi Ko is a little restaurant in a shopping plaza not far from both the Fairmont Scottsdale Princess and the Hyatt Regency Scottsdale. What makes this place stand out, in addition to the fresh and well-prepared sushi, are the unusual items that sometimes appear on the menu—fresh sardine sushi, monkfish paté, and dynamite green mussels (mussels baked with mushrooms and mayonnaise—sounds strange, but tastes great).

9301 E. Shea Blvd., no. 126, in the Mercado del Rancho shopping plaza. 𝒞 480/860-2960. Reservations recommended for dinner. Main courses $5–$12 lunch, $9.50–$19 dinner. AE, DC, DISC, MC, V. Mon–Thurs 11:30am–2pm and 5:30–10pm; Fri 11:30am–2pm and 5:30–10:30pm; Sat 5:30–10:30pm; Sun 5:30–9:30pm.

Thaifoon 🛫🛫 THAI   This may not exactly be traditional Thai food, but it sure is good. Thaifoon merges a hip upscale setting with flavorful Thai cuisine at economical prices. In fact, the food here is so good, you'll likely find yourself coming back repeatedly to try more dishes. The *tom kha gai* soup here may not be traditional, but it's the best we've ever had. Likewise, the Pattaya prawns are packed with lively flavors—plus, the dish has more prawns than we've seen at this price since the last time we were in Thailand. Don't miss the great tropical cocktails.

At the Shops at Gainey Village, 8777 N. Scottsdale Rd. 𝒞 **480/998-0011.** Call ahead to be put on waiting list. Main courses $8–$15. AE, MC, V. Sun–Thurs 11am–10pm; Fri–Sat 11am–11pm.

Tortilla Factory 🛫 MEXICAN   Moderately priced Mexican restaurants abound in Phoenix and Scottsdale, but this is one of the most enjoyable. Located in an old house surrounded by attractive patios and citrus trees that bloom in winter and spring, this place stays busy due to its creative Mexican fare and its lively bar scene (more than 100 premium tequilas are available). As you enter the restaurant grounds, you might see someone making the tortillas of the day. These tortillas come in a dozen different flavors, and will arrive at your table accompanied by chile-flavored butter. The rich tortilla soup and the tequila-lime salad make good starters. Among the entrees, we're big fans of the pork chops crusted with ancho chile powder and raspberry sauce.

6910 E. Main St. 𝒞 **480/945-4567.** www.oldtowntortillafactory.com. Reservations recommended (Fri–Sat reservations accepted only for parties of 8 or more). Main courses $9–$29. AE, DC, DISC, MC, V. Sun–Thurs 5–10pm; Fri–Sat 5–11pm (Sat drinks and appetizers 1–5pm).

Veneto Trattoria Italiana ⭐ VENETIAN ITALIAN   This pleasantly low-key bistro, specializing in the cuisine of Venice, serves simple and satisfying "peasant food" (surprising, since the owner formerly ran the restaurant at the Giorgio Armani boutique in Beverly Hills). *Baccala mantecato* (creamy fish mousse on grilled polenta, made with dried salt cod soaked in milk overnight) may sound unusual, but it's absolutely heavenly. Other good bets include the salad of thinly sliced smoked beef, shaved Parmesan, and arugula. For a finale, the *semifreddo con frutta secca,* a partially frozen meringue with dry fruits in a pool of raspberry sauce, has an intoxicating texture. There's outdoor seating on the patio (where you almost forget you're in a shopping mall) and a welcoming bistro ambience inside.

6137 N. Scottsdale Rd., in Hilton Village. ⓒ 480/948-9928. www.venetotrattoria. com. Reservations recommended. Main courses $13–$23. AE, DC, DISC, MC, V. Mon–Sat 11:30am–2:30pm and 5–10pm.

INEXPENSIVE

Author's Café ⭐ MIDDLE EASTERN/PASTRIES   Located just around the corner from the west end of Scottsdale's Main Street Arts and Antiques District, this little place serves a limited menu of salads and pita sandwiches, but these are only preludes to the real reason to come here—the desserts. Cases are filled with towering cakes and divinely decadent pastries; come early in the week for the best and freshest selection. This cafe is also a forum for self-published authors and schedules readings and other entertainment Tuesday through Saturday nights.

4014 N. Goldwater Blvd., no. 104. ⓒ 480/481-3998. Main courses $7–$10. MC, V. Mon–Thurs 9am–10pm; Fri–Sat 9am–11pm.

El Guapo's Taco Shop & Salsa Bar *Finds* MEXICAN   *Guapo* means "handsome," which certainly doesn't refer to this nondescript little hole-in-the-wall taco shop, but might refer to Danny, the proprietor. The tacos—among them mahimahi, carne asada, and marinated pork—are prepared without the standard lettuce and tomatoes, so you can build your own by liberally dousing your order with salsa and vegetable toppings from the salsa cart. El Guapo also serves cheese crisps, burritos, and nachos. Try the armadillo eggs—jalapeño peppers stuffed with cheese and deep-fried. There are about half a dozen tables packed into the little space; if you can squeeze your way up to the order counter, you'll be glad you found this place.

3015 N. Scottsdale Rd. (in Plaza 777). ⓒ 480/423-8385. Main dishes $2–$8. AE, MC, V. Mon–Sat 10am–8pm.

El Paso Barbeque Company 𝔄 BARBECUE   This is Scottsdale-style barbecue, with an upscale cowboy decor and a bar with two noisy TVs that can make for difficult conversation. But hey, if you're not in a romantic mood, this place is worth the trip for some lip-smacking barbecue, which runs the gamut from ribs to smoked chicken to more uptown dishes such as barbecued salmon and prime rib. The pulled pork with a smoky sauce and fresh coleslaw is scrumptious. There's also a wide variety of sandwiches, which makes this a good lunch spot or place to get carryout.

8220 N. Hayden Rd. ℭ **480/998-2626.** www.elpasobarbeque.com. Reservations accepted for parties of 8 or more. Main courses $6–$17. AE, DC, MC, V. Sun–Thurs 11am–10pm; Fri–Sat 11am–11pm.

Garlic's Pasta and Bread Company AMERICAN/ITALIAN This popular lunch spot is tucked into the back of the same shopping center that houses the more upscale Roy's. Although you could conceivably grab an early dinner here, this is first and foremost a great spot for a quick lunch if you happen to be cruising Scottsdale Road at midday. Creative sandwiches are the big attraction, but there are also pasta salads, soups, and even brick-oven pizzas.

At the Scottsdale Seville shopping center, 7001 N. Scottsdale Rd. ℭ **480/ 368-9699.** Reservations not accepted. Main courses $5–$7. AE, DISC, MC, V. Mon–Sat 9am–6pm.

Los Olivos 𝔄 MEXICAN   Los Olivos is a Scottsdale institution, one of the last restaurants in Old Town that dates to the days when cowboys tied up their horses on Main Street. Although the food is just standard Mexican fare, the building is a fascinating work of folk-art construction. The entrance is a bit like a cement cave, with strange figures rising up from the roof. Amazingly, this throwback to slower times is only steps away from the new Scottsdale Museum of Contemporary Art. The tortillas are made fresh on the premises.

There's another Los Olivos up in north Scottsdale, at 15544 N. Pima Rd. (ℭ **480/596-9787**).

7328 Second St. ℭ **480/946-2256.** www.losolivosrestaurant.com. Reservations recommended. Main courses $5.50–$14. AE, DC, DISC, MC, V. Sun–Thurs 11am–10pm; Fri–Sat 11am–11pm.

Oregano's Pizza Bistro PIZZA/PASTA   With very reasonable prices and a location convenient to the many shops and galleries of downtown Scottsdale, this sprawling pizza joint (two buildings and the courtyard/parking lot between) is a big hit with the area's young crowd. Both the thin-crust pizzas—topped with the likes of cilantro pesto and shredded chicken—and the Chicago stuffed pizzas are all the good things pizza should be. The menu also offers artichoke lasagna, barbecued chicken wings, salads, and even a pizza cookie for dessert. Because this is such a popular spot, expect a wait at dinner.

Other locations are in Phoenix at 130 E. Washington St. (© **602/ 253-9577**) and in Tempe at 523 W. University Dr. (© **480/ 858-0501**).

3622 N. Scottsdale Rd. (south of Indian School Rd.). © **480/970-1860**. Reservations not accepted. Main courses $5–$18. AE, DISC, MC, V. Mon–Thurs 11am–10pm; Fri–Sat 11am–11pm; Sun 11:30am–10pm.

2 North Scottsdale, Carefree & Cave Creek

VERY EXPENSIVE

Marquesa ✦✦✦ MEDITERRANEAN Marquesa, with an ambience reminiscent of an 18th-century Spanish villa, is as romantic a restaurant as you're likely to find in the valley. The menu is a contemporary interpretation of Mediterranean cuisines, and although the prices are high, we can think of few better places for a special dinner. The offerings change with the seasons, but expect them to be ripe with exotic ingredients imported from around the world, and count on almost every dish being an intensive labor of love. *Paella valenciana,* the signature dish, includes such ingredients as lobster, frogs' legs, mussels, shrimp, and cockles, and should not be missed. The Sunday "market-style" brunch is one of the best in the valley.

At the Fairmont Scottsdale Princess, 7575 E. Princess Dr. (about 12 miles north of downtown Scottsdale). © **480/585-2735**. Reservations recommended. Main courses $35–$45; champagne brunch $49; tasting menus $80. AE, DC, DISC, MC, V. Wed–Sat 6–10pm; Sun 10am–2:30pm.

EXPENSIVE

La Hacienda ✦✦ GOURMET MEXICAN As you may guess from the price range below, this is not your average taco joint. La Hacienda serves gourmet Mexican cuisine in an upscale, glamorous-but-rustic setting reminiscent of an early 1900s hacienda (stone tiled floor, Mexican glassware and crockery, a beehive fireplace). Be sure to start with the *antojitos mexicanos,* an appetizer platter that might include pork *flautas,* baked shrimp, crab cakes, and a quesadilla made with *huitlacoche,* an unusual fungus popular in Mexico. Suckling pig stuffed with chorizo is the restaurant's signature dish, but you might also encounter sautéed shrimp with smoked garlic-ancho-chile sauce or rack of lamb crusted with pumpkin seeds. Live music adds to the lively atmosphere.

At the Fairmont Scottsdale Princess, 7575 E. Princess Dr. (about 12 miles north of downtown Scottsdale). ℂ **480/585-4848.** Reservations recommended. Main courses $22–$33. AE, DC, DISC, MC, V. Thurs–Tues 6–10pm.

Michael's ⚅⚅ NEW AMERICAN/INTERNATIONAL Located in the Citadel shopping/business plaza in north Scottsdale, this restaurant was once a remote culinary outpost. But as Scottsdale's upscale suburbs march ever northward, the city has bulldozed its way to Michael's doorstep. The setting is simple yet elegant, which allows the drama of food presentation to take the fore. To start things off, do not miss the "silver spoons" hors d'oeuvres—tablespoons each containing three or four ingredients that burst with flavor. From there, it's on to such main courses as mint-tied grilled loin of lamb on a goat cheese and vegetable tart. If you can't afford a full dinner or just don't feel like a big meal, head upstairs to the bar, where there's great bar food to accompany your drinks.

8700 E. Pinnacle Peak Rd. ℂ **480/515-2575.** www.michaelsrestaurant.com. Reservations recommended. Main courses $18–$29. AE, DC, MC, V. Mon–Fri 10am–2pm and 6–10pm; Sun 10am–2pm (brunch) and 6–10pm.

Restaurant Oceana ⚅⚅ SEAFOOD   North Scottsdale is where the action is these days when it comes to new resorts, golf courses, and restaurants. Among the best of the latter is this rather small seafood establishment in an attractive shopping center that has no fewer than four upscale restaurants. As the name implies, Oceana specializes in all things finny, plus plenty of crustaceans, and everything is as fresh as it can be here in the middle of the desert. The setting and the menu are both pretty conservative, so don't expect wildly creative fare. Well-prepared standouts include the wood oven–roasted mussels, grilled rare ahi tuna, and Dungeness crab cakes. When it comes time for dessert, be sure to order a sampler plate.

At La Mirada shopping center, 8900 E. Pinnacle Peak Rd. (at Pima Rd.). ℂ **480/515-2277.** www.restaurantoceana.com. Reservations recommended. Main courses $18–$28. AE, DC, DISC, MC, V. Sun–Thurs 5:30–9pm; Fri–Sat 5:30–10pm. Closed Sun–Mon in summer.

MODERATE

Barcelona ⚅⚅ MEDITERRANEAN/NEW AMERICAN Supper clubs are all the rage in the Valley of the Sun these days, and this is the biggest and boldest of them all. The building looks to have been lifted straight out of the restaurant's namesake Spanish city, and is illuminated by giant torches. There are three bar areas, including one outdoors (for smokers), and several dining areas. The menu doesn't break any new ground, but it does have surprisingly low prices for such a gorgeous setting. The main dining room faces the bandstand and converts into a dance floor late in the evening; music is primarily jazz and Latin jazz. This is definitely a see-and-be-seen sort of place, with a brisk beautiful-people bar scene late at night. Don't miss the half-price tapas from 4 to 7pm.

There's a second Barcelona in Chandler at 900 N. 54th St. (© **480/785-9004**).

15440 Greenway-Hayden Loop. © **480/603-0370**. www.barcelonadining.com. Reservations highly recommended. Main courses $11–$25. AE, DC, DISC, MC, V. Daily 4–11pm.

The Original Crazy Ed's Satisfied Frog *(Finds* AMERICAN/ BARBECUE   Cave Creek is the Phoenix area's favorite cow-town hangout and is filled with Wild West–theme saloons and restaurants. Crazy Ed's—affiliated with the Black Mountain Brewing Company, which produces Cave Creek Chili Beer—is our favorite. You'll find Crazy Ed's in Frontier Town, a tourist-trap cow town, but don't let the location put you off. This place is just plain fun, with big covered porches and sawdust on the floor. Although the restaurant offers dishes "from the pond" and "from the chicken coop," you should stick to steaks and barbecue.

At Frontier Town, 6245 E. Cave Creek Rd., Cave Creek. © **480/488-3317**. www.satisfiedfrog.com. Reservations not accepted. Main courses $7–$17 lunch, $10–$22 dinner. AE, DISC, MC, V. Sun–Thurs 11am–9 or 10pm; Fri–Sat 11am–11pm.

Zinc Bistro *★★ (Finds* FRENCH   It may seem incongruous to find the perfect French bistro in sunny Scottsdale, and in a brand-new shopping center at that, but here it is. This place is a perfect reproduction of the sort of bistro you may have loved on your last trip to Paris. Everything is authentic, from the zinc bar to the sidewalk cafe seating to the hooks under the bar for ladies' purses. And of course there's the wait staff in their long white aprons. Try the cassoulet with duck confit, the omelet piled high with shoestring potatoes, or anything that comes with the fabulous bistro fries.

15034 N. Scottsdale Rd. © **480/603-0922**. Reservations accepted only for parties of 6 or more. Main courses $8–17 lunch, $8–$26 dinner. AE, MC, V. Daily 11am–midnight or 1am.

3 Central Phoenix & the Camelback Corridor

VERY EXPENSIVE

Mary Elaine's 𝕣𝕣𝕣 FRENCH   In the Phoenix area, Mary Elaine's is the very height of elegance and sophistication, and we say this not just because the restaurant is located on the top floor of the prestigious Phoenician resort's main building and boasts one of the best views in the valley. No, Mary Elaine's represents the pinnacle of Arizona dining for its haute cuisine, its exemplary service, and its superb table settings (Austrian crystal, French silver, and Wedgwood china). The chef focuses on the seasonal flavors of the modern French-Mediterranean kitchen. You're almost certain to encounter the signature pan-seared John Dory with fennel, artichokes, and pearl onions. Wild game, such as chateaubriand of buffalo with grilled Sonoma foie gras, shows up regularly as well. Foie gras also appears as an appetizer, here served with 100-year-old balsamic vinegar. The very extensive wine list has won numerous awards.

At the Phoenician, 6000 E. Camelback Rd. ✆ 480/423-2530. Reservations highly recommended. Jackets required for men. Main courses $41–$48; 6-course seasonal tasting menu $115 (matched wines are an additional $55). AE, DC, DISC, MC, V. Tues–Thurs 6–10pm; Fri–Sat 6–11pm.

EXPENSIVE

Eddie Matney's 𝕣𝕣 NEW AMERICAN   Eddie Matney has been on the Phoenix restaurant scene for quite a few years now, and continues to keep local diners happy with his mix of creativity and comfort. This upscale bistro is in a glass office tower at Camelback Road's most upscale corner, which means it's a popular power-lunch and business-dinner spot, but it also works well for a romantic evening out. The menu ranges far and wide for inspiration and features everything from Eddie's famous meatloaf to grilled ahi tuna. If you're not up for a splurge, you can avail yourself of the half-price happy-hour appetizers in the bar, Monday through Friday from 4 to 7pm.

2398 E. Camelback Rd. ✆ 602/957-3214. www.eddiematneys.com. Reservations recommended. Main courses $9–$15 lunch, $15–$28 dinner. AE, DISC, MC, V. Mon–Thurs 11:30am–2pm and 5–10:30pm; Fri 11:30am–2pm and 5–11:30pm; Sat 5–11:30pm.

Harris' 𝕣𝕣 STEAKHOUSE   Enormous slabs of steak, perfectly cooked and allowed to express their inner beefiness unsullied by silly sauces, are de rigueur from Manhattan to Marin County these days, and no longer is it necessary to visit some steakhouse that has aged longer than the meat it serves. Harris', smack in the middle of the bustling Camelback Corridor, is one of Phoenix's biggest contemporary steakhouses and is popular with wealthy retirees. With a Southwestern pueblo-modern styling, valet parking, and prime rib a specialty of the house, this impressive restaurant leaves no doubt that this is where the beef is. At lunch (when prices are lower), the New York steak salad with blue cheese and candied pecans fairly snaps with flavor—ask for it if you don't see it on the menu.

3101 E. Camelback Rd. ℭ **602/508-8888.** Reservations highly recommended. Main courses $8–$19 lunch, $14–$34 dinner. AE, DC, DISC, MC, V. Mon–Fri 11:30am–2pm and 5:30–10pm; Sat 5:30–10pm.

Lon's ⭐⭐ AMERICAN REGIONAL   Located in an old adobe hacienda built by cowboy artist Lon Megargee and surrounded by colorful gardens, this restaurant is one of the most "Arizonan" places in the Phoenix area, and the patio, with its views of Camelback Mountain, is so tranquil that you'll want to start shopping for a house nearby. At midday, this place is popular with both retirees and the power-lunch set, while at dinner it bustles with a wide mix of people. Dinner entrees are beautifully presented works of art, such as stuffed prawns on sun-dried tomato risotto with roasted corn and tomatillo sauce or seared duck breast on white-bean ragout with foie gras sauce. There's a good selection of wines by the glass, though they're a little on the pricey side. The bar is cozy and romantic.

At the Hermosa Inn, 5532 N. Palo Cristi Rd. ℭ **602/955-7878.** www.lons.com. Reservations recommended. Main courses $9–$14 lunch, $18–$28 dinner. AE, DC, MC, V. Mon–Fri 11:30am–2pm and 6–10pm; Sat 6–10pm; Sun 10:30am–2pm (brunch) and 6–10pm.

T. Cook's ⭐⭐⭐ MEDITERRANEAN   Ready to pop the question? On your honeymoon? Celebrating an anniversary? This is the place for you. There just isn't a more romantic restaurant in the valley. Located within the walls of the Mediterranean-inspired Royal Palms Hotel and Casitas, it's surrounded by decades-old gardens and even has palm trees growing right through the roof of the dining room. The focal point of the open kitchen is a wood-fired oven that turns out a fabulous spit-roasted chicken as well as an impressive platter of chicken, pork, and paella that's meant to be shared. T. Cook's continues to make big impressions right through to the dessert course. Although this is one of the most popular high-end restaurants in Phoenix, it manages to avoid pretentiousness.

At the Royal Palms Hotel and Casitas, 5200 E. Camelback Rd. ℂ **602/808-0766.** www.royalpalmshotel.com. Reservations highly recommended. Main courses $12–$16 lunch, $22–$30 dinner. AE, DC, DISC, MC, V. Mon–Sat 6am–2pm and 5:30–10pm; Sun 10am–2pm (brunch) and 5:30–10pm.

Roxsand ☆ NEW AMERICAN/FUSION   Located on the second floor of the exclusive Biltmore Fashion Park mall, Roxsand is a place of urban sophistication, a restaurant at which to see and be seen. The menu, a mélange of flavors from around the world, can leave you agonizing over whether to have the Moroccan *b'stilla* (braised chicken in phyllo with roasted-eggplant purée), the African spicy shrimp salad, or the curried-lamb tamale (and those are just the appetizers). Sauces sometimes lack complexity, but we do recommend the air-dried duck with pistachio onion marmalade, buckwheat crepes, and three sauces. After dinner, amble over to the awesome dessert case and feel like a kid in a candy shop.

2594 E. Camelback Rd. ℂ **602/381-0444.** Reservations recommended. Main courses $10–$13 lunch, $11–$33 dinner. AE, DC, DISC, MC, V. Mon–Thurs 11am–3pm and 5–10pm; Fri–Sat 11am–3pm and 5–10:30pm; Sun 5–9:30pm.

Vincent Guerithault on Camelback ☆☆ SOUTHWESTERN With its well-balanced blend of Southwestern and European flavors and great lunch values, this is a good place to make your initial foray into the realm of Southwestern cuisine (there are even heart-healthy dishes). Although the restaurant has an unpretentious French-country atmosphere, the cuisine is as much Southwestern as French (think sweetbreads with blue cornmeal or tequila soufflé). Grilled meats and seafood are the specialty, and might come accompanied by cilantro salsa or habanero pasta. The extensive wine list has selections from both California and France. The clientele tends to be older, well-off Phoenicians who have been eating here for years. Service has not been very good recently, but the recent renovation may jump-start better service.

3930 E. Camelback Rd. ℂ **602/224-0225.** Reservations highly recommended. Main courses $8–$10 lunch, $16–$29 dinner. AE, DC, MC, V. Mon–Fri 11:30am–2:30pm and 6–10pm; Sat 6–10pm.

Windows on the Green ☆☆ SOUTHWESTERN   Slightly more casual than Mary Elaine's, the Phoenician's premier restaurant, but no less elegant, Windows on the Green has a sweeping view of the resort's golf course. With its innovative Southwestern cuisine, this place is best appreciated by those with a taste for unusual flavor

---

(Kids) Family-Friendly Restaurants

Ed Debevic's Short Orders Deluxe (p. 85)   This replica of a classic 1950s diner is full of cool stuff, including little juke-boxes in the booths. If you have grandkids, tell them about hanging out in places like this when you were a teenager.

Organ Stop Pizza (p. 89)   A mighty Wurlitzer organ, with all the bells and whistles, entertains families while they chow down on pizza at long, communal tables.

Pinnacle Peak Patio (p. 91)   Way out in north Scottsdale, this Wild West steakhouse comes complete with cowboys, shootouts, hayrides, and live music nightly.

Rawhide Western Town (p. 106)   This place, once just a cowboy steakhouse, has become such an attraction that we've had to move it to the "Wild West Theme Towns" section of chapter 6, "Exploring," but it's still a great place to bring the kids for dinner and lots of entertainment.

Rustler's Rooste (p. 91)   Similar to Pinnacle Peak but closer to the city center, Rustler's Rooste has a slide from the lounge to the main dining room, a big patio, and live cowboy bands nightly. See if you can get your kids to try the rattlesnake appetizer—it tastes like chicken.

---

combinations. Be sure to start with the tableside guacamole and a premium margarita, before moving on to the likes of cumin-and-ancho-chile-rubbed pork chop with leek-chipotle-pepper potatoes. The wine list is chosen to complement these regional flavors. All in all, a good (though a bit pricey) introduction to Southwestern cuisine in a very classy setting.

At the Phoenician, 6000 E. Camelback Rd. ℂ **480/423-2530.** Reservations recommended. Main courses $18–$25. AE, DC, DISC, MC, V. Thurs–Mon 5–10pm.

MODERATE

Coupe des Tartes ℛ ⟨Finds⟩ COUNTRY FRENCH   Chain restaurants, theme restaurants, restaurants that are all style and little substance: Sometimes in Phoenix it seems impossible to find a genuinely homey little hole in the wall that serves good food. Coupe des Tartes is the answer to this conundrum. With barely a dozen tables and no liquor license (bring your own wine; $8 corkage fee), it's about as removed from the standard Phoenix glitz as you can get without leaving town. Start your meal with paté de campagne or brie brûlée, covered with caramelized apples. The entree menu changes regularly, but you might opt for Moroccan lamb shanks with couscous, or perhaps filet mignon with the sauce of the moment.

4626 N. 16th St. (1 block south of Camelback Rd.). ✆ **602/212-1082.** Reservations recommended. Main courses $16–$28. AE, MC, V. Tues–Sat 5:30–9:30pm.

Nonni's Kitchen 𝒜𝒜 MEDITERRANEAN   This casual neighborhood restaurant is affiliated with the ever-popular Rancho Pinot in Scottsdale, which means you can be sure the food will be great. Located in the up-and-coming Arcadia neighborhood south of Camelback Road, Nonni's is well worth searching out. The decor is minimalist Southwestern modern; the small bar area is popular with area residents. Preparations are simple and emphasize fresh (often organic) ingredients. Start off with the mesquite-grilled flatbread, and don't miss the succulent Nonni's Sunday chicken served with toasted polenta. There's a long list of wines by the glass, and right next door you'll find Postino, a great wine bar.

4410 N. 40th St. ✆ **602/977-1800.** Reservations recommended. Main courses $14–$21. AE, MC, V. Mon–Sat 5:30–10pm.

INEXPENSIVE

Ed Debevic's Short Orders Deluxe 𝒦𝒾𝒹𝓈 AMERICAN   Hidden behind the Town and Country Shopping Center, Ed's is a near-perfect replica of a classic 1950s diner, right down to the little jukeboxes in the booths. Not only does it make its own burgers, chili, and bread, but Ed's also serves the best malteds in Phoenix. The sign in the window that reads IF YOU THINK YOU HAVE RESERVATIONS, YOU'RE IN THE WRONG PLACE should give you a clue that this place is a little bit different. The place is always busy, and the waitresses are overworked (although they do break into song now and again), so don't be surprised if your waitress sits down in the booth with you to wait for your order. That's just the kind of place Ed runs, and as he says, "If you don't like the way I do things—buy me out."

2102 E. Highland Ave. ✆ **602/956-2760.** www.eddebevics.com. Reservations not accepted. Sandwiches and blue-plate specials $4–$9. AE, DISC, MC, V. Sun–Thurs 11am–9pm; Fri–Sat 11am–10pm.

5 & Diner AMERICAN   If it's 2am and you just have to have a big burger and a side of fries after a night of dancing, head for the 24-hour 5 & Diner. You can't miss it—it's the classic streamlined diner that looks as though it just materialized from New Jersey.

Other locations are in Paradise Valley at 12802 N. Tatum Blvd. (© **602/996-0033**) and in Scottsdale at Scottsdale Pavilions, 9069 E. Indian Bend Rd. (© **480/949-1957**).

5220 N. 16th St. © **602/264-5220**. www.5anddiner.com. Sandwiches/plates $4.60–$13. AE, MC, V. Daily 24 hr.

4 Downtown Phoenix

MODERATE

Alice Cooper'stown 🐦 BARBECUE   Owned by Alice Cooper himself, this sports-and-rock theme restaurant/bar is downtown's premier eat-o-tainment center. Sixteen video screens (most likely showing sports) are the centerpieces of the restaurant, but there's also an abundance of memorabilia, like guitars from Fleetwood Mac and Eric Clapton. The wait staff even wears Alice Cooper makeup. Barbecue is served in various permutations, including a huge and moderately tasty sandwich. If you were a fan, this place is a must; if you weren't, it's a miss.

101 E. Jackson St. © **602/253-7337**. www.alicecooperstown.com. Reservations not accepted. Sandwiches/barbecue $7–$20. AE, MC, V. Sun–Thurs 11am–10pm; Fri–Sat 11am–11pm.

Sam's Cafe 🐦🐦 *Value* SOUTHWESTERN   Sam's Cafe, one of only a handful of decent downtown restaurants, offers food that's every bit as imaginative, but not nearly as expensive, as that served at other (often overrated) Southwestern restaurants in Phoenix. Breadsticks with picante-flavored cream cheese, grilled vegetable tacos, and angel-hair pasta in a spicy jalapeño sauce with shrimp and mushrooms all have a nice balance of flavors. The downtown Sam's

---

Fun Fact **Forbidden City in the Desert**

So you're driving along the Loop 202 freeway near Sky Harbor Airport and this strange mirage materializes. You think you're seeing a mall-sized complex of classical Chinese buildings. Don't worry, it's not a hallucination—it's the **COFCO Chinese Cultural Center,** 668 N. 44th St. (© **602/275-8578;** www.cofco chineseculturalcr.com). This fascinating complex includes several Chinese restaurants, a Chinese garden, Asian art galleries and antiques stores, and an Asian supermarket.

Tips **For Java Hunters**

In Old Town Scottsdale, try **Desert Grind,** 7373 E. Scottsdale Mall, no. 8 (© **480/424-7678**). You'll also find fresh-roasted coffee at **Village Coffee,** 8120 N. Hayden Rd., Suite E–104 (© **480/905-0881**). Heading north up Scottsdale Road, try **Coffee Bean & Tea Leaf,** in the Shops at Gainey Village, 8877 N. Scottsdale Rd. (© **480/315-9335**). Along the Camelback Corridor, there's **Hava Java,** in the Safeway Shopping Center, Camelback Road and 32nd Street (© **602/954-9080**).

---

has a large patio that overlooks a fountain and palm garden; it stays packed with the lunchtime, after-work, and convention crowds.

Other Sam's are located in the Biltmore Fashion Park, 2566 E. Camelback Rd. (© **602/954-7100**), and in Scottsdale at 10010 N. Scottsdale Rd., at Shea Boulevard (© **480/368-2800**).

At the Arizona Center, 455 N. Third St. © **602/252-3545**. Reservations recommended. Main courses $7–$18. AE, DISC, MC, V. Mon–Thurs 11am–10pm; Fri–Sat 11am–11pm; Sun 11am–9pm.

INEXPENSIVE

Honey Bear's BBQ *Finds* BARBECUE   With a menu that's limited to pork, beef, and chicken barbecue, pork ribs, and hot links, it's almost impossible to go wrong no matter what you order at this casual, fast-food-style joint near the Heard Museum and Phoenix Art Museum. Follow it all up with sweet potato pie.

There's another location at 5012 E. Van Buren St. (© **602/ 273-9148**).

2824 N. Central Ave. © **602/279-7911**. Sandwiches and dinners $3.70–$13. AE, MC, V. Mon–Sat 10am–10pm; Sun 10am–9:30pm.

MacAlpine's Nostalgic Soda Fountain & Coffee Shoppe *Finds* AMERICAN   This is the oldest operating soda fountain in the Southwest, and it hasn't changed much since its opening in 1928. Wooden booths and worn countertops show the patina of time. Waffles are the breakfast specialty, while big burgers and sandwiches make up the lunch offerings. Wash it all down with a lemon phosphate, chocolate malted, or egg cream.

2303 N. Seventh St. © **602/262-5545**. Sandwiches/specials $3.75–$6.50. AE, MC, V. Mon–Fri 7am–2pm; Sat 10am–3pm.

Pizzeria Bianco ✧ PIZZA   Even though this historic brick building is located smack dab in the center of downtown Phoenix, the atmosphere is so cozy it feels like your neighborhood local. The wood-burning oven turns out deliciously rustic pizzas. One of our favorites is made with red onion, Parmesan, rosemary, and crushed pistachios. Don't miss the fresh mozzarella, either: Pizzeria Bianco makes its own, and it can be ordered as an appetizer or on a pizza.

At Heritage Square, 623 E. Adams St. ✆ **602/258-8300.** Reservations accepted only for parties of 6 or more. Pizzas $8.50–$12. MC, V. Tues–Sat 5–10pm; Sun 5–9pm.

5 Tempe, Mesa, South Phoenix & the Airport Area
MODERATE

House of Tricks ✧✧ NEW AMERICAN   House of Tricks is housed in a pair of old Craftsman bungalows surrounded by a garden of shady trees, and consequently, the restaurant has a completely different feel from modern Mill Avenue, Tempe's main drag, which is only 2 blocks away. This is where Arizona State University students take their parents when they come to visit, but it's also a nice spot for a romantic evening and a good place to try innovative cuisine without blowing your vacation budget. The garlic-infused Caesar salad and the house-smoked salmon with avocado, capers, and lemon cream are good bets for starters. Among the entrees, look for the pork rack with jalapeño marmalade. The grape arbor–covered patio, where there's also a shady bar, is the preferred seating area.

114 E. Seventh St., Tempe. ✆ **480/968-1114.** Reservations recommended. Main courses $6–$11 lunch, $17–$20 dinner. AE, DC, DISC, MC, V. Mon–Sat 11am–10pm.

Monti's La Casa Vieja ✧ AMERICAN   If you're tired of the glitz and glamour of the Valley of the Sun and are looking for Old Arizona, head to Monti's La Casa Vieja. The adobe building was constructed in 1873 (*casa vieja* means "old house" in Spanish) on the site of the Salt River ferry, which operated in the days when the river flowed year-round and Tempe was nothing more than a ferry crossing. Today, local families who have been in Phoenix for generations know Monti's well, and rely on the restaurant for solid meals and low prices—you can get a filet mignon for $12. The dark dining rooms are filled with memorabilia of the Old West.

1 W. Rio Salado Pkwy. (at Mill Ave.), Tempe. ✆ **480/967-7594.** www.montis.com. Reservations recommended for dinner. Main courses $8–$27. AE, DC, DISC, MC, V. Sun–Thurs 11am–10pm; Fri–Sat 11am–midnight.

INEXPENSIVE

The Farm at South Mountain *Finds* SANDWICHES/SALADS
If being in the desert has you dreaming of shady trees and green
grass, you'll enjoy this little oasis reminiscent of a New England
orchard. A rustic outbuilding has been converted to a stand-in-line
restaurant where you can order focaccia sandwiches or a delicious
pecan turkey Waldorf salad. Breakfast means baked goods such as
muffins and scones. The grassy lawn is ideal for a picnic.

Also here at the Farm, you'll find the **Garden Kitchen and
Bakery** (✆ **602/276-0601**), open Saturday and Sunday from 8am
to noon. A third restaurant, **Quiessence** (✆ **602/243-9081**), is
open Friday and Saturday, offering five-course gourmet dinners
($62) using garden produce. Reservations should be made well in
advance.

6106 S. 32nd St. ✆ **602/276-6360**. Sandwiches and salads $8.50. AE, DC, MC, V.
Tues–Sun 8am–3pm (if weather is inclement, call to be sure it's open). Take Exit
151A off I-10 and go south on 32nd St.

Los Sombreros *Finds* MEXICAN   Although this casual restaurant is located in a nondescript older shopping plaza, the crowds
waiting outside for a table should give you an idea that this is no
ordinary Mexican joint. Start with the homemade guacamole or the
quesadilla del mercado. Be sure to try the nopales salad, made with
strips of prickly-pear cactus—it's one of the best we've ever had. For
an entree, try the lamb adobo or the pumpkin seed–crusted snap-
per, and finish it all off with the *tamal de chocolate* or the cheesecake
with prickly-pear syrup.

1849 N. Scottsdale Rd. (at McKellips Rd.), Tempe. ✆ **480/994-1799**. www.los
sombreros.com. Main courses $9–$14. AE, DC, DISC, MC, V. Sun and Tues–Thurs
4:30–9pm; Fri–Sat 4:30–10pm.

Organ Stop Pizza *Kids* PIZZA   The pizza here may not be the
best in town, but the mighty Wurlitzer theater organ, the largest in
the world, sure is memorable. The massive instrument, which contains more than 5,500 pipes, has four turbine blowers to provide the
wind to create the sound, and with 40-foot ceilings in the restaurant, the acoustics are great. As you marvel at the skill of the organ-
ist, who performs songs ranging from the latest pop tunes to *The
Phantom of the Opera*, you can enjoy simple pizzas, pastas, or snack
foods such as nachos or onion rings.

1149 E. Southern Ave. (at Stapley Dr.), Mesa. ✆ **480/813-5700**. www.organstop
pizza.com. Pizzas and pastas $4.50–$15. No credit cards. Sun–Thurs 4–9pm; Fri–Sat
4–10pm.

6 Dining with a View

Different Pointe of View ⭐⭐ CLASSIC FRENCH/ REGIONAL AMERICAN   If you're staying anywhere on the north side of Phoenix or Scottsdale and crave a dining room with a view, then put the SUV in low and drive to the top of the hill at the Pointe Hilton Tapatio Cliffs Resort. Built into a mountaintop, this restaurant takes in dramatic, sweeping vistas of the city, mountains, and desert through its curving walls of glass. Come early, and you can enjoy views to the north from the lounge before heading into the south-facing dining room. The menu veers toward French haute cuisine and American fine dining: foie gras (here served with a bit of vanilla and 100-year-old balsamic vinegar), escargot in puff pastry, lobster mascarpone ravioli—you get the picture. Despite the excellent food, award-winning wine list, and live jazz Thursday through Saturday, the view steals the show.

At the Pointe Hilton Tapatio Cliffs Resort, 11111 N. Seventh St. ✆ 602/863-0912. Reservations highly recommended. Main courses $29–$40. AE, DC, DISC, MC, V. Sun–Thurs 6–9pm; Fri–Sat 6–10pm (lounge open later).

Top of the Rock ⭐⭐ NEW AMERICAN/SOUTHWESTERN Almost all of the best views in Phoenix are from expensive resort restaurants, so if you want to dine with a view of the valley, you're going to have to pay the price. For desert drama, no other view restaurant can compare with Top of the Rock, which, quite literally, is built into the top of a rocky hill looking north across the valley. Luckily, quality accompanies the high prices, and in addition to the romantic setting, you can enjoy some very creative cuisine. Among the appetizers, don't miss the honey-glazed wild boar or the ostrich medallions with fig and pine-nut ragout. The menu changes regularly, but keep an eye out for the blue corn–crusted halibut. The ambience is a little on the formal side, but you don't necessarily have to get dressed up.

At The Buttes, A Wyndham Resort, 2000 Westcourt Way, Tempe. ✆ 602/225-9000. Reservations recommended. Main courses $24–$31; Sun brunch $36. AE, DC, DISC, MC, V. Sun–Thurs 5–10pm; Fri–Sat 5–11pm; Sun 10am–1:30pm and 5–10pm.

7 Cowboy Steakhouses

Cowboy steakhouses are family restaurants that generally provide big portions of grilled steaks and barbecued ribs, outdoor and "saloon" dining, live country music, and various other sorts of entertainment. The biggest of these is **Rawhide Western Town,** a Wild

West theme park with a big steakhouse, stagecoach rides, and shootouts in the street. See p. 106 for details.

Pinnacle Peak Patio ☆ *Kids* STEAKHOUSE Once located miles out in the desert, this "Hollywood Western" steakhouse is now surrounded by some of the valley's poshest suburbs. Despite the million-dollar homes, this joint still knows how to keep the Wild West alive. Although you can indulge in mesquite-broiled steaks with all the traditional trimmings, a meal here is more an event than just an opportunity to strap on the feed bag. The real draw is all the entertainment—gunfights, cowboy bands, two-stepping, and cookouts. Also of interest are the museumlike displays of interesting collections including can openers, police badges, and license plates. Businessmen, beware! Wear a tie into this place, and you'll have it cut off and hung from the rafters.

10426 E. Jomax Rd., Scottsdale. ℂ 480/585-1599. www.pppatio.com. Reservations accepted only for parties of 8 or more. Main courses $6.50–$25; children's menu $2.50–$6.50. AE, DC, DISC, MC, V. Mon–Thurs 4–10pm; Fri–Sat 4–11pm; Sun noon–10pm. Take Scottsdale Rd. north to Thompson Peak Rd. east to Pima Rd. north to Happy Valley Rd.

Rustler's Rooste ☆ *Kids* STEAKHOUSE This location, in the middle of a sprawling golf resort, doesn't exactly seem like cowboy country. But up at the top of the hill, you'll find a fun Western-theme restaurant where you can start your meal by going down a big slide from the bar to the main dining room. While the view north across Phoenix is entertainment enough for most people, there are also bands playing for those who like to kick up their heels. If you've ever been bitten by a snake, you can exact your revenge here by ordering the rattlesnake appetizer. Follow that (if you've got the appetite of a hardworking cowpoke) with the enormous cowboy "stuff" platter consisting of, among other things, broiled steak, barbecued ribs, cowboy beans, fried shrimp, barbecued chicken, and skewered swordfish.

At the Pointe South Mountain Resort, 7777 S. Pointe Hwy., Phoenix. ℂ 602/431-6474. www.rustlersrooste.com. Reservations recommended. Main courses $13–$32. AE, DC, DISC, MC, V. Daily 5–10pm.

8 Breakfast, Brunch & Quick Bites

Most of Phoenix's best Sunday brunches are to be had at restaurants in major hotels and resorts. Among the finest are those served at **Marquesa** (at the Scottsdale Princess), **T. Cook's** (at the Royal Palms Hotel and Casitas), the **Golden Swan** (at the Hyatt Regency

Scottsdale), **Wright's** (at the Arizona Biltmore Resort & Spa), the **Terrace Dining Room** (at the Phoenician), and **Top of the Rock** (at The Buttes).

The **Desert Botanical Garden,** 1201 N. Galvin Pkwy., in Papago Park (© **480/941-1225;** www.dbg.org), serves brunch with its Music in the Garden concerts held on Sunday from September to March. Tickets are $14 and include admission to the gardens, but meals cost extra.

If your idea of the perfect breakfast is a buttery brioche and a good cup of coffee, try **Pierre's Pastry Café,** 7119 E. Shea Blvd., Scottsdale (© **480/443-2510**); desserts here are also irresistible. Along Camelback Road, in the Biltmore Plaza shopping center, try **La Madeleine,** 3102 E. Camelback Rd. (© **602/952-0349**), *the* place for a leisurely French breakfast amid antique farm implements. Other branches are at Fashion Square Mall, 7014 E. Camelback Rd., Scottsdale (© **480/945-1663**), and at Tatum and Shea boulevards in Paradise Valley (© **480/483-0730**).

For smoothies, muffins, and healthy things, try **Wild Oats Community Market,** which has stores at 3933 E. Camelback Rd. (© **602/954-0584**), in North Phoenix at 13823 N. Tatum Blvd. (© **602/953-7546**), and in Scottsdale at Shea Boulevard and Scottsdale Road (© **480/905-1441**).

6

Exploring

With its wealth of museums and galleries, its interesting architecture and its many outdoor activities, the Phoenix and Scottsdale area offers something for everyone. This chapter will guide you through the highlights, including how to get tee times at the top golf courses, where to find an excellent massage, and the best places to take kids.

1 The Desert & Its Native Cultures

Deer Valley Rock Art Center ⌖ Located in the Hedgepeth Hills in the northwest corner of the Valley of the Sun, the Deer Valley Rock Art Center preserves an amazing concentration of Native American petroglyphs, some of which date back 5,000 years. The drawings, which range from simple spirals to much more complex renderings of herds of deer, are on volcanic boulders along a quarter-mile trail. An interpretive center provides background information on this site and on rock art in general.

3711 W. Deer Valley Rd. ☎ **623/582-8007.** www.asu.edu/clas/anthropology/dvrac. Admission $4 adults, $2 seniors and students, $1 children 6–12. Oct–Apr Tues–Sat 9am–5pm, Sun noon–5pm; May–Sept Tues–Fri 8am–2pm, Sat 9am–5pm, Sun noon–5pm. Closed major holidays. Take Deer Valley Rd. exit off I-17 on the north side of Phoenix and go west to just past 35th Ave.

Desert Botanical Garden ⌖⌖⌖ Located in Papago Park adjacent to the Phoenix Zoo and devoted exclusively to cacti and other desert plants, this botanic garden displays more than 20,000 plants from all over the world. The Plants and People of the Sonoran Desert Trail is the state's best introduction to ethnobotany (human use of plants) in the Southwest. Along the trail are interactive displays that demonstrate how Native Americans once used wild and cultivated plants. You can make a yucca-fiber brush and practice grinding corn and mesquite beans. At the Center for Desert Living, there are demonstration gardens and an energy- and water-conservation research house. On the Harriet K. Maxwell Desert Wildflower Trail, you'll find an ever-changing palette of colorful

Phoenix, Scottsdale & the Valley of the Sun Attractions

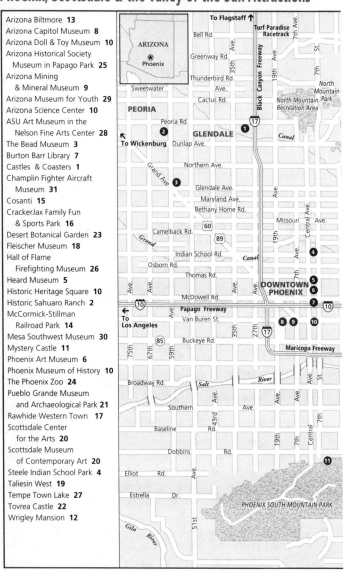

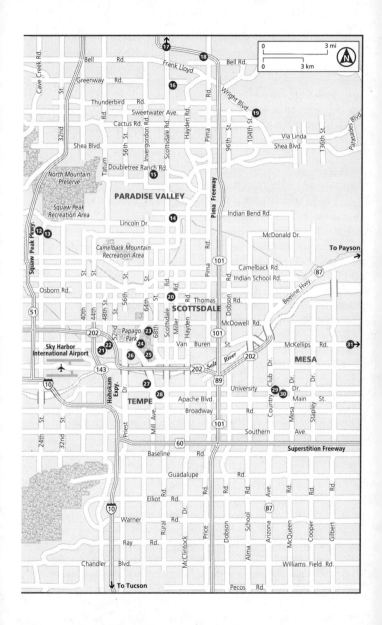

wildflowers throughout much of the year. If you come late in the day, you can stay until after dark and see night-blooming flowers and dramatically lit cacti. A cafe on the grounds serves surprisingly good food. In spring and fall, there are concerts in the garden. In early December, during *Las Noches de las Luminarias,* the gardens are lit at night by luminarias (candles inside small bags).

At Papago Park, 1201 N. Galvin Pkwy. ✆ **480/941-1225.** www.dbg.org. Admission $7.50 adults, $6.50 seniors, $4 students 13–18, $3.50 children 5–12. Oct–Apr daily 8am–8pm; May–Sept daily 7am–8pm. Closed July 4 and Christmas. Bus: 3.

Heard Museum 👁👁👁   The Heard Museum is one of the nation's finest museums dealing exclusively with Native American cultures and is an ideal introduction to the indigenous peoples of Arizona. The extensive exhibit *Native Peoples of the Southwest* examines the culture of each of the major tribes of the region and includes a Navajo hogan, an Apache wickiup, and a Hopi corn-grinding display. In the Katsina Doll Gallery, you'll get an idea of the number of different kachina spirits that populate the Hopi and Zuni religions, while the Crossroads Gallery offers a fascinating look at contemporary Native American art. On many weekends, there are performances by singers and dancers, and throughout the week, artists demonstrate their work. Guided tours are offered daily. The annual **Indian Fair and Market,** held on the first weekend in March, includes traditional dances along with arts and crafts.

The museum also operates **Heard Museum North,** at El Pedregal Festival Marketplace, 34505 N. Scottsdale Rd., in Carefree. This gallery features changing exhibits and is open Monday through Saturday from 10am to 5:30pm and Sunday from noon to 5pm. Admission is $2 for adults and $1 for children 4 to 12.

2301 N. Central Ave. ✆ **602/252-8848.** www.heard.org. Admission $7 adults, $6 seniors, $3 children 4–12. Daily 9:30am–5pm. Closed major holidays. Bus: Blue (B), Red (R), O.

Pueblo Grande Museum and Archaeological Park   Located near Sky Harbor Airport and downtown Phoenix, the Pueblo Grande Museum and Archaeological Park houses the ruins of an ancient Hohokam village that was one of several villages along the Salt River between A.D. 300 and 1400. Sometime around 1450, this and other villages were mysteriously abandoned. Some speculate that drought and a buildup of salts from irrigation water reduced the fertility of the soil and forced the people to seek more productive lands. The small museum displays many of the artifacts that have been dug up on the site. Although these exhibits are actually more interesting than the ruins themselves, there are also some reconstructed and furnished Hohokam-style houses that give a good idea of how the Hohokam lived. The museum sponsors interesting workshops (some just for kids), demonstrations, and tours (including petroglyph hikes). In mid-December, the **Pueblo Grande Museum Indian Market** is held at South Mountain Park Activity Center Complex, 10919 S. Central Ave. It is the largest market of its kind in the state and features more than 450 Native American artisans.

4619 E. Washington St. (between 44th and 48th sts.). ℭ **877/706-4408** or 602/495-0901. www.pueblogrande.com. Admission $2 adults, $1.50 seniors, $1 children 6–17; free on Sun. Mon–Sat 9am–4:45pm; Sun 1–4:45pm. Closed major holidays. Bus: Yellow (Y).

2 Museums

ART MUSEUMS

ASU Art Museum in the Nelson Fine Arts Center ⟡
Although it isn't very large, this museum is memorable for its innovative architecture and excellent temporary exhibitions. With its purplish-gray stucco facade and pyramidal shape, the stark and angular building conjures up images of sunsets on desert mountains. The entrance is down a flight of stairs that leads to a cool underground garden area. Inside are galleries for crafts, prints, contemporary art, and Latin American art, along with outdoor sculpture courts and a gift shop. The collection of American art includes works by Georgia O'Keeffe, Edward Hopper, and Frederic Remington. Definitely a must for both art and architecture fans.

10th St. and Mill Ave., Tempe. ℭ **480/965-2787.** http://asuartmuseum.asu.edu/home.html. Free admission. Tues 10am–9pm (10am–5pm in summer); Wed–Sat 10am–5pm; Sun 1–5pm. Closed major holidays. Bus: Red (R), Yellow (Y), 66, or 72.

Fleischer Museum   This museum, located in an office park in north Scottsdale, was the first gallery in the country to focus on what is now known as the California School of American Impressionism. Unless you're a serious student of art (or a big fan of Impressionism), you probably won't want to make a special drive out here. If you're out this way anyway (perhaps to do a tour at Frank Lloyd Wright's nearby Taliesin West), you may want to stop by.

17207 N. Perimeter Dr., Scottsdale. ℭ **480/585-3108.** www.fleischer.org. Admission $5 adults, free for children under 18. Daily 10am–4pm. Closed major holidays. Located just north of Frank Lloyd Wright Blvd. and east of Greenway-Hayden Loop.

Phoenix Art Museum ⭐⭐   This is one of the largest art museums in the Southwest, and within its labyrinth of halls and galleries is a respectable collection that spans the major artistic movements from the Renaissance to the present. Exhibits cover decorative arts, historic fashions, Spanish-colonial furnishings and religious art, and, of course, works by members of the Cowboy Artists of America. The collection of modern and contemporary art is particularly good, with works by Diego Rivera, Frida Kahlo, Pablo Picasso, Alexander Calder, Henry Moore, Georgia O'Keeffe, Henri Rousseau, and Auguste Rodin. The popular Thorne Miniature Collection consists of tiny rooms on a scale of 1 inch to 1 foot. Through June 2003, you can take in the unusual *Vital Forms: American Art and Design in the Atomic Age, 1940–1960.* If you're in town between January 26 and May 4, 2003, be sure to plan a visit to the *El Greco to Picasso* exhibit.

1625 N. Central Ave. (at McDowell Rd.). ✆ **602/257-1222.** www.phxart.org. Admission $7 adults, $5 seniors and students, $2 children 6–17; free on Thurs. Tues–Wed and Fri–Sun 10am–5pm; Thurs 10am–9pm. Closed major holidays. Bus: Blue (B), Red (R), O.

Scottsdale Museum of Contemporary Art ⭐⭐   Scottsdale may be obsessed with art featuring lonesome cowboys and solemn Indians, but this boldly designed museum makes it clear that patrons of contemporary art are also welcome here. Cutting-edge art, from the abstract to the absurd, fills the galleries, with exhibits rotating every few months. In addition to the main building, there are several galleries in the adjacent Scottsdale Center for the Arts, which also has a pair of Dale Chihuly art-glass installations. The museum shop is excellent.

7374 E. Second St., Scottsdale. ✆ **480/994-ARTS.** www.scottsdalearts.org. Admission $7 adults, $5 students, free for children under 15; free on Thurs. Tues–Wed and Fri–Sat 10am–5pm; Thurs 10am–8pm; Sun noon–5pm. Bus: 41, 50, 72. Also accessible via Scottsdale Round Up shuttle bus.

HISTORY MUSEUMS & HISTORIC LANDMARKS

Arizona Capitol Museum ⭐   In the years before Arizona became a state, the territorial capital moved from Prescott to Tucson, then back to Prescott, before finally settling in Phoenix. In 1898, a stately territorial capitol building was erected (with a copper roof to remind the local citizenry of the importance of that metal in the Arizona economy). Atop this copper roof was placed the statue *Winged Victory,* which still graces the old capitol building today. This building no longer serves as the actual state capitol, but has been restored to the way it appeared in 1912, the year Arizona became a state. Among the rooms on view are the senate and house chambers, as well as the governor's office. Excellent exhibits provide interesting perspectives on early Arizona events and lifestyles.

1700 W. Washington St. © 602/542-4675. www.lib.az.us/museum. Free admission. June–Dec Mon–Fri 8am–5pm; Jan–May Mon–Fri 8am–5pm, Sat 10am–3pm. Closed state holidays. Bus: Yellow (Y).

Arizona Historical Society Museum in Papago Park ⚐   This museum, at the headquarters of the Arizona Historical Society, focuses its well-designed exhibits on the history of central Arizona. Temporary exhibits on the lives and works of the people who helped shape this region are always highlights of a visit. An interesting permanent exhibit features life-size statues of everyday people from Arizona's past (a Mexican miner, a Chinese laborer, and so on). Quotes relate their individual stories, while props reveal what items they might have possessed during their days in the desert.

1300 N. College Ave. (just off Curry Rd.), Tempe. © 480/929-0292. www.tempe.gov/ahs. Free admission. Tues–Sat 10am–4pm; Sun noon–4pm. Bus: 66.

Historic Heritage Square   Although the city of Phoenix was founded in 1870, much of its history has been obliterated. If you have an appreciation for old homes and want a glimpse of how Phoenix once looked, stroll around this collection of some of the city's few remaining 19th-century Victorian-style houses, which stand here on the original town site. Today, they house museums, restaurants, and gift shops. The Eastlake Victorian Rosson House, furnished with period antiques, is open for tours. The Silva House contains exhibits on life in the late 19th century. The Stevens-Haustgen House offers a gift shop, while the Stevens House features the Arizona Doll and Toy Museum. The Forest's Carriage House has a gift shop and ticket window for the Rosson House tours. The Teeter House now serves as a Victorian tearoom; the old Baird Machine Shop contains Pizzeria Bianco; and the Thomas House is home to Bar Bianco.

115 N. Sixth St., at Monroe. © 602/262-5029 or 602/262-5071. www.rosson housemuseum.org. Rosson House tours $4 adults, $3 seniors, $1 children 6–12. Hours vary for each building; call for information. Bus: Red (R), Yellow (Y), 0.

Historic Sahuaro Ranch   Phoenix and neighboring valley communities started out as farming communities, but today there's little sign of this early agricultural heritage. This historic ranch in Glendale is one noteworthy exception. With its tall date palms, resident peacocks, and restored farmhouse, Sahuaro Ranch is a great introduction to what life was like here in the late 19th and early 20th centuries. The old fruit-packing shed now serves as a gallery hosting temporary exhibits; tours of the main house are offered.

9802 N. 59th Ave. (at Mountain View Rd.), Glendale. ✆ **623/939-5782.** www.sahuaroranch.org. Admission $3, free for children 12 and under. Wed–Fri 10am–2pm; Sat 10am–4pm; Sun noon–4pm. Bus: 59.

Phoenix Museum of History ✪   Located adjacent to Heritage Square in downtown Phoenix, this state-of-the-art museum is one of the anchors of the city's downtown revitalization plan. It presents an interesting look at the history of a city that, to the casual visitor, might not seem to *have* any history. Interactive exhibits make this place much more interesting than your average local history museum. One unusual exhibit explores how "lungers" (tuberculosis sufferers) inadvertently helped found the tourism industry in Arizona. There's also an exhibit on ostrich ranching.

105 N. Fifth St. ✆ **602/253-2734.** www.pmoh.org. Admission $5 adults, $3.50 seniors and students, $2.50 children 6–12. Mon–Sat 10am–5pm; Sun noon–5pm. Closed major holidays. Bus: Red (R) or Yellow (Y).

Pioneer Arizona Living History Museum ✪   This museum, 20 miles north of downtown Phoenix, includes nearly 30 original and reconstructed buildings, as well as costumed interpreters practicing traditional frontier activities. Among the buildings are a carpentry shop, miner's cabin, stagecoach station, one-room schoolhouse, opera house, church, and Victorian home. Gunfights are staged daily; there's also a variety of special events year-round.

3901 W. Pioneer Rd. (take Exit 225 off I-17). ✆ **623/465-1052.** Admission $7 adults, $6 seniors, $5 students, $4 children 3–5. Oct–May Wed–Sun 9am–5pm; June–Sept Wed–Sun 9–3pm.

SCIENCE & INDUSTRY MUSEUMS

Arizona Science Center ✪ *Kids*   Aimed primarily at children but also loads of fun for adults, this hands-on facility is one of the anchors of Phoenix's ongoing downtown renewal. You'll find state-of-the-art interactive exhibits covering a variety of topics, from the human body to life in the desert. There's a huge ant farm, a virtual-reality game that puts you inside a video game, a flight simulator, and a cloud maker. The science center also includes a planetarium and a large-screen theater, both of which carry additional charges.

600 E. Washington St. ✆ **602/716-2000.** www.azscience.org. Admission $8 adults, $6 seniors and children 3–12. Planetarium and film combination tickets also available. Daily 10am–5pm. Closed Thanksgiving and Christmas. Bus: Red (R), Yellow (Y), 0.

Mesa Southwest Museum ★★ *Kids* This is one of the best museums in the valley, and with its wide variety of exhibits it will appeal to people with a range of interests. For the kids, there are animated dinosaurs on an indoor "cliff" with a roaring waterfall, plus plenty of dinosaur skeletons. Also of interest are an exhibit on movies that have been filmed in the state, a display on Arizona mammoth kill sites, some old jail cells, and a walk-through mine mock-up with exhibits on the Lost Dutchman Mine. There's also a mock-up of a pre-Columbian temple and an artificial cave filled with beautiful mineral specimens.

53 N. MacDonald St. (at First St.), Mesa. ℂ 480/644-2230. www.ci.mesa.az.us. Admission $6 adults, $5 seniors and students, $3 children 3–12. Tues–Sat 10am–5pm; Sun 1–5pm. Closed major holidays. Bus: Red (R).

A MUSEUM MISCELLANY: PLANES, FLAMES & MORE

Arizona Mining & Mineral Museum Arizonans have been romancing the stones for more than a century at colorfully named mines, such as the Copper Queen, Sleeping Beauty, and Lucky Boy. Out of such mines have come countless tons of copper, silver, and gold, as well as beautiful minerals with tongue-twisting names. Chalcanthite, chalcoaluminate, and chrysocolla are just some of the richly colored minerals on display at this small downtown museum. Rather than playing up the historical or profit-making side of the industry, exhibits focus on the amazing variety of Arizona minerals. Displays have a dated feel, but the beauty of the minerals makes this an interesting stop for aspiring rockhounds.

1502 W. Washington St. ℂ 602/255-3795. www.admmr.state.az.us. Free admission. Mon–Fri 8am–5pm; Sat 11am–4pm. Closed state holidays. Bus: Yellow (Y).

The Bead Museum You'll see beads and body adornments from around the world at this interesting little museum in the Glendale antiques district. Ancient and modern beads are on display, and exhibits focus on such subjects as beaded bags and prayer beads.

5754 W. Glenn Dr., Glendale. ℂ 623/931-2737. www.thebeadmuseumaz.com. Admission $4 adults, $2 children. Mon–Sat 10am–5pm (Thurs until 8pm); Sun 11am–4pm. Bus: Yellow (Y).

Champlin Fighter Aircraft Museum This aeronautical museum, dedicated exclusively to fighter planes and the fighter aces who flew them, houses aircraft from World Wars I and II, the Korean War, the Vietnam War, and Desert Storm, with a strong emphasis on the wood-and-fabric biplanes and triplanes of World

War I. Jet fighters from more recent battles include a MiG-15, a MiG-17, and an F4 Phantom. Also here at Falcon Field is the **Arizona Wing,** 2017 N. Greenfield Rd. (© **480/924-1940;** www. arizonawingcaf.org), which showcases the restored *Sentimental Journey,* a 1944 B-17 bomber.

At Falcon Field Airport, 4636 Fighter Aces Dr. (off McKellips Rd.), Mesa. © **480/ 830-4540.** Admission $6.50 adults, $3.50 children 5–12. Apr 15–Sept 15 daily 8:30am–3:30pm; Sept 16–Apr 14 daily 10am–5pm. Take Ariz. 202 (Red Mountain Fwy.) east to the McKellips Rd. exit; continue slightly more than 6 miles east on McKellips Rd.

Hall of Flame Firefighting Museum ✮ *(Kids)* The world's largest firefighting museum houses a fascinating collection of vintage fire engines. The displays range from a 1725 English hand pumper to several classic engines from the 20th century. All are beautifully restored and, of course, fire-engine red (mostly). In all, there are more than 90 vehicles on display.

At Papago Park, 6101 E. Van Buren St. © 602/275-3473. www.hallofflame.org. Admission $5 adults, $4 seniors, $3 students 6–17, $1.50 children 3–5. Mon–Sat 9am–5pm; Sun noon–4pm. Closed New Year's Day, Thanksgiving, and Christmas. Bus: 3.

3 Architectural Highlights

Arizona Biltmore This resort hotel, although not designed by Frank Lloyd Wright, shows the famed architect's hand in its distinctive cast-cement blocks. It also displays sculptures, furniture, and stained glass designed by Wright. The best way to soak up the ambience of this exclusive resort (if you aren't staying here) is over dinner, a cocktail, or tea. To learn more about the building, reserve ahead for a tour, given Saturday at 2:30pm.

2400 E. Missouri Ave. © 602/955-6600. Tours $10 (free for resort guests).

Burton Barr Library This library is among the most daring pieces of public architecture in the city, and no fan of futuristic art or science fiction should miss it. The five-story cube is partially clad in enough ribbed copper sheeting to produce roughly 17.5 million pennies. The building's design makes use of the desert's plentiful sunshine to provide light for reading, but also incorporates computer-controlled louvers and shade sails to reduce heat and glare.

1221 N. Central Ave. © 602/262-4636. www.phoenixpubliclibrary.org. Free admission. Mon–Thurs 9am–9pm; Fri–Sat 9am–6pm; Sun noon–9pm. Bus: Red (R), Blue (B), or 0.

Cosanti   This complex of cast-concrete structures served as a prototype and learning project for architect Paolo Soleri's much grander Arcosanti project, currently under construction north of Phoenix (p. 149). It's here at Cosanti that Soleri's famous bells are cast, and most weekday mornings you can see the foundry in action.

6433 E. Doubletree Ranch Rd., Scottsdale. © **800/752-3187** or 480/948-6145. www.cosanti.com. Suggested donation $1. Mon–Sat 9am–5pm; Sun 11am–5pm. Closed major holidays. Drive 1 mile west of Scottsdale Rd. on Doubletree Ranch Rd.

Mystery Castle ✦ *Finds*   Built for a daughter who longed for a castle more permanent than those built in sand at the beach, Mystery Castle is a wondrous work of folk-art architecture. Boyce Luther Gulley, who had come to Arizona in hopes of curing his tuberculosis, constructed the castle during the 1930s and early 1940s using stones from the property. The resulting 18-room fantasy has 13 fireplaces, parapets, and many other unusual touches. Tours are usually led by Mary Lou Gulley, the daughter for whom the castle was built.

800 E. Mineral Rd. © **602/268-1581**. Admission $5 adults, $4 seniors, $2 children 5–14. Thurs–Sun 11am–4pm. Closed July–Sept. Take Central Ave. south to Mineral Rd. (2 miles south of Baseline Rd.) and turn east.

Taliesin West ✦✦✦   Frank Lloyd Wright fell in love with the Arizona desert and, in 1937, built Taliesin West as a winter camp that served as his office and school. Today, the buildings of Taliesin West are the headquarters of the Frank Lloyd Wright Foundation and School of Architecture.

Tours explain the campus buildings and include a general introduction to Wright and his theories of architecture. Wright believed in using local materials in his designs, and this is in evidence at Taliesin West, where local stone was used for building foundations. He developed a number of innovative methods for dealing with the extremes of the desert climate, such as sliding wall panels to let in varying amounts of air and light.

Architecture students, and anyone interested in the work of Wright, will enjoy browsing the excellent books in the gift shop. Expanded Insight Tours ($18–$22), behind-the-scenes tours ($35), guided desert walks ($20), apprentice shelter tours ($30), and night hikes ($25) are also available at certain times of year. Call ahead for schedule information.

12621 Frank Lloyd Wright Blvd. (at 114th St.), Scottsdale. © **480/860-2700**, ext. 494 or 495. www.franklloydwright.org. Basic tours: Nov–Apr $16 adults, $14 seniors and students, $3 children 4–12; June–Sept $12.50 adults, $10 students and seniors, $4.50 children 4–12. Oct–May daily 10am–4pm; June–Sept daily 9am–4pm. Closed Tues–Wed in July and Aug, Easter, Thanksgiving, Christmas, New Year's Day, and occasional special events. From Scottsdale Rd., go east on Shea Blvd. to 114th St., then north 1 mile to the entrance road.

Tovrea Castle   Another architectural confection of the Phoenix landscape, Tovrea Castle has been likened to a giant wedding cake and is currently under renovation. Although the gardens should be open by the time you read this, work on the building itself may continue through 2003. Call for updates.

5041 E. Van Buren St. ✆ **602/262-6412.** Call for hours and admission information.

Wrigley Mansion   This elegant mansion was built by chewing-gum magnate William Wrigley, Jr., between 1929 and 1931 as a present for his wife, Ada. Designed with Italianate styling, the many levels and red-tile roofs make it seem like an entire village. The mansion is now a National Historic Landmark, with the interior restored to its original elegance. Although this is currently a private club, tours are offered, and membership is only $10 and basically gives you dining privileges, although you can eat here once without having a membership.

2501 E. Telawa Trail. ✆ **602/955-4079.** www.wrigleymansionclub.com. Tours $10; Tues and Thurs 10am and 3pm. Call for restaurant hours and reservations.

4 Wild West Theme Towns

Since there are more Ford Mustangs than wild mustangs around Phoenix and Scottsdale, you'll have to get out of town way before sundown if you want a taste of the Old West. Scattered around the valley are a handful of Hollywood-style cow towns that are basically just tourist traps, but, hey, if you've got the kids along, you owe it to them to visit at least one of these places.

Cave Creek, founded as a gold-mining camp in the 1870s, is the last of the valley towns that still has some semblance of Wild West character, but this is rapidly fading as area real-estate prices skyrocket and Scottsdale's population center moves ever northward. Still, you'll see several steakhouses, saloons, and shops selling Western and Native American crafts and antiques. The main family attraction is a place called **Frontier Town,** which is right on Cave Creek Road in the center of town. It's a sort of mock-up cow town that is home to the Black Mountain Brewing Company, which brews Cave Creek Chili Beer. You can try this fiery beer at **Crazy Ed's Satisfied Frog Restaurant and Saloon,** located here in Frontier Town (p. 80). To learn more about the history of this area,

Carefree Living

Carefree, a planned community established in the 1950s and popular with retirees, is much more subdued than its neighbor Cave Creek, which effects a sort of Wild West character. Ho Hum Road and Easy Street are just two local street names that reflect the sedate nature of Carefree, home to the exclusive **Boulders** resort, which boasts a spectacular setting, a Golden Door Spa, and a couple of excellent restaurants. On Easy Street, in what passes for Carefree's downtown, you'll find one of the world's largest sundials. The dial is 90 feet across, and the gnomon (the part that casts the shadow) is 35 feet tall. From the gnomon hangs a colored-glass star, and in the middle of the dial is a pool of water and a fountain. Also downtown is a sort of reproduction Spanish-village shopping area, and just south of town, adjacent to the Boulders, is the upscale **El Pedregal Festival Marketplace** shopping center, with interesting boutiques, galleries, and a few restaurants.

stop in at the **Cave Creek Museum,** at Skyline Drive and Basin Road (© **480/488-2764**). It's open from October to May, Wednesday through Sunday from 1 to 4:30pm; admission is by donation.

Goldfield Ghost Town *(Kids* Over on the east side of the valley, just 4 miles northeast of Apache Junction, you'll find a reconstructed 1890s gold-mining town. Although it's a bit of a tourist trap—gift shops, an ice-cream parlor, and the like—it's also home to the **Superstition Mountain Museum** (© **480/983-4888**), which has interesting exhibits on the history of the area. Of particular note is the exhibit on the Lost Dutchman gold mine, perhaps the most famous mine in the country despite the fact that its location is unknown. Goldfield Ghost Town and Mine Tours provides guided tours of the gold mine beneath the town. The Superstition Scenic Narrow Gauge Railroad circles the town, and the **Goldfield Livery** (© **480/982-0133**) offers horseback riding and carriage rides. If you're here at lunchtime, you can get a meal at the steakhouse/saloon.

Ariz. 88, 4 miles northeast of Apache Junction. © 480/983-0333. www.goldfield ghosttown.com. Museum admission $2 adults, $1.50 seniors, 75¢ children; train rides $4 adults, $3.50 seniors, $2 children 5–12; mine tours $5 adults, $3 children 6–12; 1-hr. horseback rides $20. Daily 10am–5pm. Saloon open daily 10am–8pm.

Rawhide Western Town 🌟 *Kids*   Sure, it's a tourist trap, but this fake cow town is so much fun and such a quintessentially Phoenician experience that no family should get out of town without first moseying down the dusty streets of Rawhide. Those streets are lined with lots of tourist shops and plenty of places for refreshments, including a steakhouse that was the original reason for Rawhide's existence. Rawhide is run like other amusement parks in that you buy a bunch of $1 tickets and then trade those tickets for performances (stunt shows, gunfights) and activities (stagecoach rides, train rides, mechanical-bull rides). Half-hour horseback rides are $15, and there are also cowboy cookouts ($30 adults, $18 children) with hayrides and live music. Friday nights bring bull-riding exhibitions.

23023 N. Scottsdale Rd. (4 miles north of Bell Rd.), Scottsdale. ℂ 480/502-1880. www.rawhide.com. Individual tickets $1 (rides and performances require 1–4 tickets); all-day passes $15. Hours vary; call for details.

5 Parks & Zoos

Perhaps the most unusual park in the Phoenix metro area centers on **Tempe Town Lake** (ℂ 480/350-8625; www.tempe.gov/rio), which was created in 1999 by damming the Salt River with inflatable dams. With its construction, Tempe now has a 2-mile-long lake for boating, and lining the north and south shores are bike paths and parks. The best lake access is at Tempe Town Beach, at the foot of the Mill Avenue Bridge. Here, you can rent kayaks and other small boats, and even take a brief excursion with **Rio Lago Cruise** (ℂ 480/517-4050), which charges $6 for adults, $5 for seniors and children 6 to 12, and $4 for children 5 and under. Tempe Town Lake is the focus of a grand development plan known as the Rio Salado Project, which will eventually include a hotel and other commercial facilities. Until then, most of the south shore of the lake is a barren wasteland waiting to be developed.

Among the city's most popular parks are its natural areas and preserves. These include Phoenix South Mountain Park, Papago Park, Phoenix Mountains Preserve (site of Squaw Peak), North Mountain Preserve, North Mountain Recreation Area, and Camelback Mountain–Echo Canyon Recreation Area. For more information on these parks, see "Hiking," "Bicycling," and "Horseback Riding" under "Outdoor Pursuits," below.

Not far from downtown Phoenix is the **Steele Indian School Park,** at Third Street and Indian School Road (ℂ 602/495-0937). This is a recently opened park that, as its name implies, was once an

Indian school. Several of the old buildings are still standing, but it's the many new fountains, gardens, and interpretive displays that make this such a fascinating place. A stop here can easily be combined with a visit to the nearby Heard Museum.

Out of Africa Wildlife Park *(Kids)*   At this small wildlife park northeast of Scottsdale, animals put on shows for you. The most popular performances are those in the park's swimming pool. You've probably never seen tigers, wolves, and bears having so much fun in the water. Call for a schedule of daily shows.

9736 N. Fort McDowell Rd., Scottsdale. ℂ **480/837-7779.** www.outofafrica.com. Admission $15 adults, $14 seniors, $6.95 children 3–12. Oct–May Tues–Sun 9:30am–5pm; June–Sept Wed–Fri 4–9:30pm, Sat 9:30am–9:30pm, Sun 9:30am–5pm. Closed Thanksgiving and Christmas. Take Ariz. 87 northeast from Mesa and 2 miles past Shea Blvd.; turn right on Fort McDowell Rd.

The Phoenix Zoo *(Kids)*   Forget about polar bears and other cold-climate creatures; this zoo focuses its attention primarily on animals that come from climates similar to that of the Phoenix area (the rainforest exhibit is a definite exception). Most impressive of the displays are the African savanna and the baboon colony. The Southwestern exhibits are also of interest, as are the giant Galápagos tortoises. All animals are kept in naturalistic enclosures, and what with all the palm trees and tropical vegetation, the zoo sometimes manages to make you forget that this really is the desert.

At Papago Park, 455 N. Galvin Pkwy. ℂ **602/273-1341.** www.phoenixzoo.org. Admission $12 adults, $9 seniors, $5 children 3–12. Sept–Apr daily 9am–5pm; June–Aug daily 7am–8pm. Closed Christmas. Bus: 3, FLASH Lite.

6 Especially for Kids

In addition to the following suggestions, kids are likely to enjoy the Arizona Science Center, the Mesa Southwest Museum, the Hall of Flame Firefighting Museum, Out of Africa Wildlife Park, the Phoenix Zoo and the Wild West theme towns—all described in detail above.

Arizona Doll & Toy Museum   This small museum is located in the historic Stevens House on Heritage Square in downtown Phoenix. The miniature classroom peopled by doll students is a favorite exhibit. With dolls dating from the 19th century, this is a definite must for doll collectors.

Heritage Square, at Seventh and Monroe sts. ℂ **602/253-9337.** Admission $2.50 adults, $1 children. Sept–July Tues–Sat 10am–4pm; Sun noon–4pm. Closed Aug. Bus: Red (R), Yellow (Y), 0.

Arizona Museum for Youth Using both traditional displays and participatory activities, this museum allows children to explore the fine arts and their own creativity. It's housed in a refurbished grocery store, which for past exhibits has been transformed into a zoo, a ranch, and a foreign country. Exhibits are geared mainly to toddlers through 12-year-olds, but all ages can work together to experience the activities. In 2002, this museum moved into temporary quarters, but by the time you read this, it should be back at the address listed here. The new and expanded museum is scheduled to reopen sometime in 2003; call ahead to be sure of the address.

35 N. Robson St. (between Main and First sts.), Mesa. 📞 480/644-2467. www.ci.mesa.az.us/amfy. Admission $2.50, free for children under 2. Fall–spring Sun and Tues–Fri 1–5pm, Sat 10am–5pm; summer Tues–Sat 9am–5pm, Sun 1–5pm. Closed Thanksgiving, Christmas, Dec 31–Jan 1, and for 2 weeks between exhibits. Bus: Red (R).

Castles & Coasters Located adjacent to Metrocenter, one of Arizona's largest shopping malls, this small amusement park boasts an impressive double-loop roller coaster, plenty of tamer rides, four 18-hole miniature-golf courses, and a pavilion full of video games.

9445 N. Metro Pkwy. E. 📞 602/997-7575. www.castlesncoasters.com. Ride and game prices vary; $7 minimum; all-day passes $18–$23. Open daily (hours change seasonally; call ahead). Bus: Red (R) or 27.

CrackerJax Family Fun & Sports Park Two miniature-golf courses are the main attractions here, but you'll also find a driving range, a professional putting course for grown-up golfers, batting cages, go-cart tracks, a bumper-boat lagoon, and a video-game arcade.

16001 N. Scottsdale Rd. (¼ mile south of Bell Rd.), Scottsdale. 📞 480/998-2800. Activity prices vary; multiple-activity passes $12–$19 adults, $11–$15 children. Open daily (hours change seasonally; call ahead). Bus: 72.

McCormick-Stillman Railroad Park If you or your kids happen to like trains, you won't want to miss this park. On the grounds are restored cars and engines, two old railway depots, model railroad layouts operated by a local club, and, best of all, a $5/12$-scale model railroad that takes visitors around the park. There's also a 1929 carousel and a general store.

7301 E. Indian Bend Rd. (at Scottsdale Rd.), Scottsdale. 📞 480/312-2312. www.therailroadpark.com. Train and carousel rides $1; museum admission $1 adults, free for children 12 and under. Hours vary with the season; call for schedule. Bus: 72.

7 Organized Tours & Excursions

The Valley of the Sun is a sprawling, often congested place, and if you're unfamiliar with the area, you may be surprised at how great the distances are. If map reading and urban navigation are not your strong points, consider taking a guided tour. There are numerous companies offering tours of both the Valley of the Sun and the rest of Arizona. However, tours of the valley tend to include only brief stops at highlights.

BUS TOURS   **Gray Line of Phoenix** (© 800/732-0327 or 602/495-9100; www.graylinearizona.com) is one of the largest tour companies in the valley. It offers a 4-hour tour of Phoenix and the Valley of the Sun for $41; reservations are necessary. The tour points out such local landmarks as the state capitol, Heritage Square, Arizona State University, and Old Town Scottsdale.

GLIDER RIDES   The thermals that form above the mountains in the Phoenix area are ideal for sailplane (glider) soaring. On the south side of the valley in Maricopa, **Arizona Soaring** (© 520/568-2318, or 480/821-2903 for information; www.azsoaring.com) offers sailplane rides as well as instruction. A basic 20-minute flight is $75; for $120 to $150, you can take an aerobatic flight with loops, rolls, and inverted flying. To reach the airstrip, take I-10 east to Exit 162A, go 15 miles, turn west on Ariz. 238, and continue 6½ miles. On the north side of the valley, there's **Turf Soaring School,** 8700 W. Carefree Hwy., Peoria (© 602/439-3621; www.turf soaring.com), which charges $85 for a basic flight and $125 for an aerobatic flight. This outfitter also offers flights for two people ($150), although your combined weight can't exceed 300 pounds. Reservations are a good idea at either place.

HOT-AIR BALLOON RIDES   The still morning air of the Valley of the Sun is perfect for hot-air ballooning, and because of the stiff competition, prices are among the lowest in the country— between $125 and $150 per person for a 1- to 1½-hour ride. Companies to try include **Over the Rainbow** (© 602/225-5666; www.letsgoballooning.com), **Zephyr Balloon/A Aerozona Adventure** (© 888/991-4260 or 480/991-4260; www.azballoon. com), **Adventures Out West** (© 800/755-0935 or 602/996-6100; www.adventuresoutwest.com), and **Unicorn Balloon Company** (© 800/468-2478 or 480/991-3666; www.unicornballoon.com).

Tips Top Gun

Ever wanted to be a fighter pilot? Well, at **Fighter Combat International** (© **866/FLY-HARD** or 480/279-1881; www.fighter combat.com), you can find out if you've got the right stuff. This company, which operates out of the Williams Gateway Airport in Mesa, offers a variety of adventure aerobatic flights, including mock dogfights. Best of all, you get to fly the plane up to 75% of the time and learn how to do loops, rolls, spins, and other aerobatic moves. Flights start at $265; for the full *Top Gun* experience, you'll have to shell out $955.

JEEP TOURS   After spending a few days in Scottsdale, you'll likely start wondering where the desert is. Well, it's out there, and the easiest way to explore it is to book a Jeep tour. Most hotels and resorts have particular companies they work with, so start by asking your concierge. Alternatively, you can contact one of the following companies. Most will pick you up at your hotel, take you off through the desert, and maybe even let you try panning for gold or shooting a six-gun. Rates are around $75 to $85 for a 4-hour tour. Companies include **Western Events** (© **800/567-3619** or 480/860-1777; www.azdesertmountain.com) and **Arizona Bound Tours** (© **480/994-0580;** www.arizonabound.com).

If you want to really impress your friends when you get home, you'll need to try something a little different. How about a Hummer tour? Sure, a Hummer is nothing but a Jeep on steroids, but these military-issue off-road vehicles still turn heads. Contact **Desert Storm Hummer Tours** (© **480/922-0020;** www.dshummer.com), which charges $90 for a 4-hour tour, or **Extreme Hummer Adventures** (© **602/402-0584;** www.stellaradventures.com), which charges $115 for a basic 4-hour tour and $155 for its extreme tour.

SCENIC FLIGHTS   If you're short on time but want to see the Grand Canyon, book an air tour in a small plane. **Westwind Tours** (© **888/869-0866** or 480/991-5557; www.westwindaviation.com) charges $270 to $320 for its Grand Canyon tours and $390 to $445 for its Monument Valley tours. This company flies out of the Deer Valley Airport in the northwest part of the valley.

8 Outdoor Pursuits

BICYCLING   Although the Valley of the Sun is a sprawling place, it's mostly flat and has numerous paved bike paths, which makes bicycling a breeze as long as it isn't windy or in the heat of summer. **Wheels 'n Gear,** in the Plaza Del Rio Shopping Center, 7607 E. McDowell Rd., Scottsdale (© 480/945-2881), rents cruisers for $15 per day and mountain bikes for $30 to $55 per day. Mountain-biking trail maps are also available.

Among the best mountain-biking spots in the city are Papago Park (at Van Buren St. and Galvin Pkwy.), Phoenix South Mountain Park (use the entrance off Baseline Rd. on 48th St.), and North Mountains Preserve (off Seventh St. between Dunlap Ave. and Thunderbird Rd.). With its rolling topography and wide dirt trails, Papago Park is the best place for novice mountain-bikers to get in some desert riding (and the scenery here is great). For hard-core pedalers, Phoenix South Mountain Park is the place to go. The National Trail is the ultimate death-defying ride here, but there are lots of trails for intermediate riders, including the Desert Classic Trail and the short loop trails just north of the parking area at the 48th Street entrance. North Mountain is another good place for intermediate riders.

There's also plenty of good mountain biking up in the Cave Creek area, where you can rent a bike for $35 a day at **Cave Creek Bike & Tours Co.,** 6149 Cave Creek Rd. (© 480/488-5261). This shop also offers guided mountain-bike tours for $65. If you'd like a guide for some of the best biking in the desert, contact **Desert Biking Adventures** (© 888/249-BIKE or 602/320-4602), which leads 2-, 3-, and 4-hour tours (and specializes in downhill rides). Prices range from $70 to $97. If you plan to do much mountain biking around the state, pick up a copy of *Fat Tire Tales and Trails,* by Cosmic Ray.

If you'd rather confine your cycling to a paved surface, there's no better route than Scottsdale's **Indian Bend Wash greenbelt,** a paved path that extends for more than 10 miles along Hayden Road (from north of Shea Blvd. to Tempe). The Indian Bend Wash pathway can be accessed at many points along Hayden Road. At the south end, the path connects to paved paths on the shores of Tempe Town Lake and provides easy access to Tempe's Mill Avenue shopping district.

CANOEING/KAYAKING Maybe these sports don't jump to mind when you think of the desert, but there are indeed rivers and lakes here (they happen to be some of the best places to see wildlife). **Permagrin Canoeing & Kayak Outfitters,** 107 E. Broadway Rd., Suite B, Tempe, AZ 85282 (© **480/755-1924;** www.go-perma grin.com), offers various canoeing and kayaking courses.

GOLF With nearly 200 courses in the Valley of the Sun, golf is just about the most popular sport in Phoenix and one of the main reasons people flock here in winter. Sunshine, spectacular views, and the company of coyotes, quails, and doves make playing a round of golf here a truly memorable experience.

Despite the number of courses, it can still be difficult to get a tee time on any of the more popular courses (especially during the months of Feb, Mar, and Apr). If you're staying at a resort with a course, be sure to make your tee-time reservations at the same time you make your room reservations. If you aren't staying at a resort, you might still be able to play a round on a resort course if you can get a last-minute tee time. Try one of the tee-time reservations services below.

The only thing harder than getting a winter or spring tee time in the valley is facing the bill at the end of your 18 holes. Greens fees at most public and resort courses range from $90 to $170, with the top courses often charging $200 or more. Municipal courses, on the other hand, charge under $40. You can save money on many courses by opting for twilight play, which usually begins between 1 and 3pm.

You can get more information on Valley of the Sun golf courses from the **Greater Phoenix Convention & Visitors Bureau,** 50 N. Second St. (© **877/225-5749** or 602/254-6500; www.phoenix cvb.com). In addition, you can pick up the *Official Arizona Golf Guide & Directory* at visitor bureaus, golf courses, and many hotels and resorts.

It's a good idea to make reservations well in advance. You can avoid the hassle of booking tee times yourself by contacting **Golf Xpress** (© **800/878-8580** or 602/404-GOLF; www.azgolfxpress. com), which can make reservations farther in advance than you could if you called the golf course directly, and can sometimes get you lower greens fees as well. This company also makes hotel reservations, rents golf clubs, and provides other assistance to golfers visiting the valley. For last-minute reservations, call **Stand-by Golf** (© **800/655-5345** or 480/874-3133).

The many resort courses are the favored fairways of valley visitors. For spectacular scenery, the two Jay Morrish–designed 18-hole courses at the **Boulders** ⚐⚐, N. Scottsdale Road and Carefree Highway, Carefree (© **800/553-1717** or 480/488-9009), just can't be beat. Given the option, play the South Course, and watch out as you approach the tee box on the seventh hole—it's a real heart-stopper. Tee times for nonresort guests are very limited in winter and spring, and you'll pay $220 for a round. In summer, you can play for as little as $110 (just be sure you get the earliest possible tee time and bring plenty of water).

Jumping over to Litchfield Park, on the far west side of the valley, there's the **Wigwam Golf and Country Club** ⚐, 300 Wigwam Blvd. (© **623/935-3811**), which has, count 'em, three championship 18-hole courses. The Gold Course is legendary, but the Blue and Red courses are also worth playing. These are traditional courses for purists who want vast expanses of green rather than cactus and boulders. In high season, greens fees are $120 for any of the three courses ($60 for twilight play on the Blue or Red course; $24–$37 in summer). Reservations for nonguests can be made no more than 7 days in advance.

Way over on the east side of the valley at the foot of the Superstition Mountains is the **Gold Canyon Golf Resort** ⚐, 6100 S. Kings Ranch Rd., Gold Canyon (© **800/827-5281;** www.gcgr. com), which has been rated the best public course in the state and has three of the state's best holes—the second, third, and fourth on the visually breathtaking, desert-style Dinosaur Mountain course. Greens fees on this course range from $135 to $165 in winter and from $50 to $65 in summer. The Sidewinder course is more traditional and less dramatic, but much more economical. Greens fees are $75 to $95 in winter and $40 to $50 in summer. Reserve a week in advance. It's well worth the drive.

If you want a traditional course that has been played by presidents and celebrities alike, try to get a tee time at one of the two 18-hole courses at the **Arizona Biltmore Country Club,** 24th Street and Missouri Avenue (© **602/955-9655**). The courses here are more relaxing than challenging, good to play if you're not yet up to par. Greens fees are $165 in winter and spring, $48 in summer. Reservations can be made up to a month in advance. There's also a championship 18-hole putting course.

Of the two courses at the **Camelback Golf Club,** 7847 N. Mockingbird Lane (© **800/24-CAMEL** or 480/596-7050), the

Resort Course underwent a $16-million redesign a few years ago and has new water features and bunkers. The Club Course is a links-style course with great mountain views and lots of water hazards. Resort Course greens fees are $125 to $145 in winter and $40 to $50 in summer; Club Course fees are $90 to $105 in winter and $30 to $40 in summer. Reservations can be made up to 30 days in advance.

Set at the base of Camelback Mountain, the **Phoenician Golf Club,** 6000 E. Camelback Rd. (© **800/888-8234** or 480/423-2449; www.thephoenician.com), at the valley's most glamorous resort, has 27 holes that mix traditional and desert styles. Greens fees for nonresort guests are $170 in winter and spring, and $90 in summer, and can be made a week in advance.

Of the valley's many daily-fee courses, it's the two 18-hole courses at **Troon North Golf Club** ✿✿✿, 10320 E. Dynamite Blvd., Scottsdale (© **888/TROON-US** or 480/585-7700; www.troon golf.com), seemingly just barely carved out of raw desert, that garner the most local accolades. This is the finest example of a desert course that you'll find anywhere in the state, and with five tee boxes on each hole, golfers of all levels will be thoroughly challenged. Greens fees are $240 in winter and spring, $75 to $90 in summer. Reservations are taken up to 30 days in advance.

If you want to swing where the pros do, beg, borrow, or steal a tee time on the Tom Weiskopf and Jay Morrish–designed Stadium Course at the **Tournament Players Club (TPC) of Scottsdale** ✿✿, 17020 N. Hayden Rd. (© **888/400-4001** or 480/585-4334; www.playatpc.com), which hosts the Phoenix Open. The 18th hole has standing room for 40,000 spectators, but hopefully there won't be that many around the day you double bogey on this hole. The TPC's second 18, the Desert Course, is actually a municipal course, thanks to an agreement with the landowner, the Bureau of Land Management. Stadium course fees are $214 in winter and spring, $91 in summer. Desert Course fees are down around $50.

The **Kierland Golf Club,** 15636 Clubgate Dr., Scottsdale (© **888/TROON-US** or 480/922-9283; www.troongolf.com), which was designed by Scott Miller and consists of three nine-hole courses that can be played in combination, is another much-talked-about local daily-fee course. It's affiliated with the new Westin Kierland Resort, which was still under construction at press time. Greens fees are $130 to $155 in winter, $55 to $65 in summer. Book up to 60 days in advance.

The Pete Dye–designed **ASU-Karsten Golf Course,** 1125 E. Rio Salado Pkwy., Tempe (© **480/921-8070;** www.asukarsten.com), part of Arizona State University, is also highly praised and a very challenging training ground for top collegiate golfers. Greens fees are $69 to $93 in winter and $28 to $38 in summer. Phone reservations are taken up to 14 days in advance; online reservations are taken up to 30 days in advance.

If you're looking for good value in traditional or links-style courses, try the Legacy Golf Resort, Stonecreek Golf Club, or Ocotillo Golf Resort. The **Legacy Golf Resort,** 6808 S. 32nd St. (© **602/305-5550;** www.legacygolfresort.com), which was the site of the 2000 LPGA tournament, is a fairly forgiving course on the south side of the valley. Greens fees are $140 in winter and $45 to $65 in summer.

Stonecreek Golf Club, 4435 E. Paradise Village Pkwy. (© **602/953-9111**), conveniently located in Paradise Valley close to Old Scottsdale, is named for the artificial stream that meanders through the course. Greens fees are $105 to $125 in winter and $40 to $45 in summer.

Ocotillo Golf Resort, 3751 S. Clubhouse Dr., Chandler (© **480/917-6660**), in the southeast part of the valley, has three nine-hole courses centered around 95 acres of man-made lakes, and that means a lot of challenges. Greens fees are $155 in winter and $45 in summer.

If you want to take a crack at a desert-style course or two but don't want to take out a second mortgage, try Dove Valley Ranch Golf Club, Rancho Mañana Golf Club, or the new We-Ko-Pa Golf Club. **Dove Valley Ranch Golf Club,** 33244 N. Black Mountain Pkwy., Cave Creek (© **480/488-0009;** www.dovevalleyranch.com), designed by Robert Trent Jones, Jr., was voted Arizona's best new public course when it opened in 1998. It's something of a merger of desert and traditional styles. Greens fees are $90 to $130 in winter and $30 to $55 in summer.

Rancho Mañana Golf Club, 5734 E. Rancho Mañana Blvd., Cave Creek (© **480/488-0398;** www.ranchomanana.com), on the north side of the valley near the Boulders, makes a good introduction to desert-style courses, as it's not as challenging as some other options in the area. Greens fees are $110 to $135 in winter and down around $50 in summer.

We-Ko-Pa Golf Club, 18200 East Toh Vee Circle, Fountain Hills (© **866/660-7700** or 480/836-1453; www.wekopa.com), one of the newest courses in the area, is located off the Beeline Highway (Ariz. 87) on the Fort McDowell Yavapai Nation in the northeast corner of the valley, and has been getting rave reviews since it opened. The course name is Yavapai for "Four Peaks," which is the mountain range you'll be marveling at as you play. The desert crowds the fairways here, so make sure you keep your ball on the grass. Greens fees are $155 to $165 in winter and $45 to $55 in summer. Reservations are taken up to 30 days in advance.

Of the municipal courses in Phoenix, **Papago Golf Course,** 5595 E. Moreland St. (© **602/275-8428**), at the foot of the red-sandstone Papago Buttes, offers fine views and a killer 17th hole. This is such a great course that it's used for Phoenix Open qualifying. **Encanto Golf Course,** 2745 N. 15th Ave. (© **602/253-3963**), is the third-oldest course in Arizona and, with its wide fairways and lack of hazards, is very forgiving. **Cave Creek Golf Course,** 15202 N. 19th Ave. (© **602/866-8076**), in north Phoenix, is another good, economical choice. In winter, greens fees at these three municipal courses are $26 on weekdays and $35 on weekends. Keep in mind that rates don't include a golf cart, which is another $18 to $22 in winter.

HIKING Several mountains around Phoenix, including Camelback Mountain and Squaw Peak, have been set aside as parks and nature preserves, and these natural areas are among the city's most popular hiking spots. The city's largest nature preserve, **Phoenix South Mountain Park** (© **602/495-0222**), said to be the largest city park in the world, contains miles of hiking, mountain-biking, and horseback-riding trails, and the views of Phoenix (whether from along the National Trail or from the parking lot at the Buena Vista Overlook) are spectacular, especially at sunset. To reach the park's main entrance, drive south on Central Avenue, which leads right into the park. Once inside the park, turn left on Summit Road and follow it to the Buena Vista Lookout, which provides a great view of the city and is the trail head for the National Trail. If you hike east on this trail for 2 miles, you'll come to an unusual little tunnel that makes a good turnaround point. Another stretch of the National Trail can be accessed from the 48th Street park entrance, which is reached by driving through the property of the Pointe South Mountain Resort.

Another good place to get in some relatively easy and convenient hiking is at **Papago Park** (© **602/262-4837**), home to the Desert Botanical Garden, the Phoenix Zoo, and the fascinating Hole in the

Rock (a red-rock butte with a large opening in it). There are both paved and dirt trails within the park; the most popular hikes are around the Papago Buttes (park on West Park Dr.) and up onto the rocks at Hole in the Rock (park past the zoo at the information center).

Perhaps the most popular hike in the city is the trail to the top of **Camelback Mountain,** in **Echo Canyon Recreation Area** (② **602/ 256-3220**), near the boundary between Phoenix and Scottsdale. This is the highest mountain in Phoenix, and the 1¼-mile Summit Trail to the top is very steep, yet on any given day there will be iron-men and ironwomen nonchalantly jogging up and down to stay fit. At times, it almost feels like a health-club singles scene. The views are the finest in the city. To reach the trail head, drive up 44th Street until it becomes McDonald Drive, turn right on East Echo Canyon Drive, and continue up the hill until the road ends at a parking lot, which is often full. Don't attempt this one in the heat of the day, and bring at least a quart of water.

At the east end of Camelback Mountain is the Cholla Trail, which, at 1¾ miles in length, isn't as steep as the Summit Trail (at least not until you get close to the summit, where the route gets steep, rocky, and quite difficult). The only parking for this trail is along Invergordon Road at Chaparral Road, just north of Camelback Road (along the east boundary of the Phoenician resort). Be sure to park in a legal parking space and watch the hours that parking is allowed. There's a good turnaround point about 1½ miles up the trail, and great views down onto the fairways of the golf course at the Phoenician.

Squaw Peak, in the **North Mountains Preserve** (② **602/ 262-7901**), offers another aerobic workout of a hike and has views almost as spectacular as those from Camelback Mountain. The round-trip to the summit is 2½ miles. Squaw Peak is reached from Squaw Peak Drive off Lincoln Drive between 22nd and 23rd streets.

For much less vigorous hiking, try **North Mountain Park** (② **602/262-7901**), in North Mountain Preserve. This natural area, located on either side of Seventh Street between Dunlap Avenue and Thunderbird Road, has more flat hiking than Camelback Mountain or Squaw Peak.

HORSEBACK RIDING Even in the urban confines of the Phoenix metro area, people like to play at being cowboys. Keep in mind that most stables require or prefer reservations. Since any guided ride is going to lead you through interesting desert scenery, your best bet is to pick a stable close to where you're staying. Two area resorts—Pointe Hilton Tapatio Cliffs Resort and Pointe South Mountain Resort—have on-site riding stables.

On the south side of the city, try **Ponderosa Stables,** 10215 S. Central Ave. (© **602/268-1261**), or **South Mountain Stables,** 10005 S. Central Ave. (© **602/276-8131**), both of which lead rides into South Mountain Park and charge $20 per hour. These stables also offer fun dinner rides ($24) to the T-Bone Steakhouse, where you buy your own dinner before riding back under the stars. In the Scottsdale area, **MacDonald's Ranch,** 26540 N. Scottsdale Rd. (© **480/585-0239;** www.macdonaldsranch.com), charges $24 for a 1-hour ride and $30 for a 1½-hour ride.

On the north side of the valley, **Cave Creek Outfitters,** off Dynamite Boulevard on 144th Street (© **480/471-4635**), offers 2-hour rides for $60. **Trail Horse Adventures,** Spur Cross Road, Cave Creek (© **800/723-3538** or 928/282-7252; www.trailhorse adventures.com), does everything from 1-hour rides ($30) to overnight trips ($250).

On the east side of the valley, on the southern slopes of the Superstitions, is one of the most famous names in Arizona horseback riding, **Don Donnelly Stables,** 5580 S. Kings Ranch Rd., Gold Canyon (© **800/346-4403** or 480/982-7822; www.don donnelly.com), which charges $27 for a 1-hour ride and $133 per person for an overnight trip (4-person minimum).

IN-LINE SKATING In the Scottsdale area, you can rent in-line skates at **Scottsdale Sidewalk Surfer,** 2602 N. Scottsdale Rd. (© **480/994-1017**). Rates are $2 an hour or $10 per day. Staff members can point you toward nearby spots that are good for skating. Adjacent to the shop is one of the best places, the **Indian Bend Wash greenbelt,** which extends for more than 10 miles. It runs parallel to Hayden Road in Scottsdale from north of Shea Boulevard to Washington Street.

TENNIS Most major hotels in the area have tennis courts, and there are several tennis resorts around the valley. Noteworthy tennis-oriented resorts in the Phoenix/Scottsdale area are the Phoenician, the Radisson Resort Scottsdale, Copperwynd Country Club & Inn, the Fairmont Scottsdale Princess, the Pointe South Mountain Resort, and the Pointe Hilton Tapatio Cliffs Resort. If you're staying someplace without a court, try the **Scottsdale Ranch Park,**

10400 E. Via Linda, Scottsdale (© **480/312-7774**). Court fees range from $3 to $6 per hour.

WATER PARKS At **Waterworld Safari Water Park,** 4243 W. Pinnacle Peak Rd. (© **623/581-8446;** www.golfland-sunsplash. com/phoenix), you can free-fall down the Kilimanjaro speed slide or catch a gnarly wave in the wave pool. **Mesa Golfland-Sunsplash,** 155 W. Hampton Ave., Mesa (© **480/834-8318;** www.golfland-sunsplash.com/mesa), has a wave pool and a tunnel called the Black Hole. **Big Surf,** 1500 N. McClintock Rd. (© **480/947-2477;** www.golfland-sunsplash.com/tempe), has a wave pool, a speed slide, and more.

All three of these parks charge about $17 for adults ($12 after 3 or 4pm) and $14 for children 4 to 11. Waterworld Safari Water Park and Mesa Golfland-Sunsplash are open from around Memorial Day to Labor Day, Monday through Thursday from 10am to 8pm, Friday and Saturday from 10am to 9pm, and Sunday from 11am to 7pm. Big Surf is open Monday through Saturday from 10am to 6pm and Sunday from 11am to 7pm.

WHITE-WATER RAFTING & TUBING The desert may not seem like the place for white-water rafting, but up in the mountains to the northeast of Phoenix, the **Upper Salt River** still flows wild and free and offers some exciting rafting. Most years from about late February to late May, snowmelt from the White Mountains turns the river into a Class III and IV river filled with exciting rapids (sometimes, however, there just isn't enough water). Companies operating full-day, overnight, and multi-day rafting trips on the Upper Salt River (conditions permitting) include **Far Flung Adventures** (© **800/359-2627;** www.farflung.com), **Canyon Rio Rafting** (© **800/272-3353**), and **Mild to Wild Rafting** (© **800/ 567-6745;** wwwmild2wildrafting.com). Prices range from $100 to $114 for a day trip. Rafting trips are also available on the upper Salt River east of Phoenix.

Tamer river trips can be had from **Salt River Recreation** (© **480/984-3305;** www.saltrivertubing.com), which has its head-quarters 20 miles northeast of Phoenix on Power Road at the inter-section of Usery Pass Road in Tonto National Forest. For $12, the company will rent you a large inner tube and shuttle you by bus upriver for the float down. The inner-tubing season runs from May to September.

9 Spectator Sports

Phoenix has gone nuts over pro sports and is now one of the few cities in the country with all four of the major sports teams (baseball, basketball, football, and hockey). Add to this baseball's spring training, professional women's basketball, three major golf tournaments, tennis tournaments, the annual Fiesta Bowl college football classic, and ASU football, basketball, and baseball, and you have enough action to keep even the most rabid sports fans happy. The all-around best month to visit is March, when you could feasibly catch baseball's spring training, the Suns, the Coyotes, and ASU basketball and baseball, as well as the Franklin Templeton Tennis Classic and the PING Banner Health LPGA Tournament.

Call **Ticketmaster** (℃ **480/784-4444;** www.ticketmaster.com) for tickets to most of the events below. For sold-out events, try **Tickets Unlimited** (℃ **800/289-8497** or 602/840-2340; www. ticketsunlimitedinc.com) or **Ticket Exchange** (℃ **800/800-9811** or 602/254-4444).

AUTO RACING   At the **Phoenix International Raceway,** S. 115th Avenue and Baseline Road, Avondale (℃ **602/252-2227;** www.phoenixinternationalraceway.com), there's NASCAR and Indy car racing on the world's fastest 1-mile oval. Tickets range from $15 to $45.

BASEBALL   The **Arizona Diamondbacks** (℃ **888/777-4664** or 602/514-8400; www.azdiamondbacks.com) surprised most of the nation by beating the New York Yankees in the last inning of the last game of the 2001 World Series. Such an edge-of-the-seat upset makes for rabidly loyal fans for this young team, which plays in downtown Phoenix at the state-of-the-art Bank One Ballpark (BOB). The ballpark's retractable roof allows for comfortable play during the blistering summers, and makes this one of the only enclosed baseball stadiums with natural grass. Tickets to ball games are available through the Bank One Ballpark ticket office and cost between $6 and $75. **Bank One Ballpark Tours** (℃ **602/ 462-6799**) cost $6 for adults, $4 for children 7 to 12, and $2 for children 4 to 6.

For decades, it has been **spring training** that gives Phoenix its annual shot of baseball, and don't think that the Cactus League's preseason exhibition games will be any less popular just because the Diamondbacks won the World Series and are around all summer. Spring-training games may rank second only to golf in popularity with winter visitors to the valley. Nine major league baseball teams have spring-training camps around the valley during March and April, and exhibition games are scheduled at six different stadiums. Tickets cost $3 to $20. Get a schedule from a visitor center, check the *Arizona Republic* while you're in town, or go to www.cactus-league.com. Games often sell out, especially on weekends, so be sure to order tickets in advance. The spring-training schedule for 2003 should be out by December 2002.

Teams training in the valley include the **Anaheim Angels,** Tempe Diablo Stadium, 2200 W. Alameda Dr. (48th St. and Broadway Rd.), Tempe (© 602/438-9300 or 480/784-4444; www.angels baseball.com); **Chicago Cubs,** HoHoKam Park, 1235 N. Center St., Mesa (© 800/905-3315 or 480/964-4467; www.cubspring training.com); **Milwaukee Brewers,** Maryvale Baseball Park, 3600 N. 51st Ave., Phoenix (© 623/245-5500; www.milwaukeebrewers. com); **Oakland Athletics,** Phoenix Municipal Stadium, 5999 E. Van Buren St., Phoenix (© 800/905-3315 or 602/392-0217; www.oaklandathletics.com); **San Diego Padres,** Peoria Sports Complex, 16101 N. 83rd Ave., Peoria (© 623/878-4337 or 480/784-4444; www.padres.com); **San Francisco Giants,** Scottsdale Stadium, 7408 E. Osborn Rd., Scottsdale (© 480/ 990-7972; www.sfgiants.com); and **Seattle Mariners,** Peoria Sports Complex, 16101 N. 83rd Ave., Peoria (© 623/878-4337 or 480/784-4444; www.seattlemariners.com). As of 2003, the **Kansas City Royals** and the **Texas Rangers** will have moved their spring training camps to the Phoenix area, specifically to a new stadium complex in the northwest valley community of Surprise.

BASKETBALL The NBA's **Phoenix Suns** play at the America West Arena, 201 E. Jefferson St. (© **800/4-NBA-TIX** or 602/379-SUNS; www.suns.com). Tickets cost $10 to $95. Suns tickets are hard to come by; if you haven't planned ahead, try contacting the box office the day before or the day of a game to see if tickets have been returned. Otherwise, you'll have to try a ticket agency and pay a premium.

Phoenix also has a WNBA team, the **Phoenix Mercury** (© **602/ 252-WNBA** or 602/379-7800; www.wnba.com/mercury), which plays at the America West Arena between late May and mid-August. Tickets cost $8 to $38.

FOOTBALL The **Arizona Cardinals** (© **800/999-1402** or 602/379-0102; www.azcardinals.com) are in the planning process for building a new stadium. However, negotiations over where it will be located have dragged on for years; at press time, no decision had yet been made. So, until a new stadium is constructed, the Cardinals will continue to play at Arizona State University's Sun Devil Stadium, which is also home to the Fiesta Bowl Football Classic. Tickets cost $25 to $80 and go on sale in mid-July.

While the Cardinals get to use Sun Devil Stadium, this field really belongs to Arizona State University's **Sun Devils** (✆ 480/965-2381). Tickets for the Devils range from $24 to $40.

Despite the desert heat and presence of a baseball team, Phoenicians don't give up football just because it's summer. The **Arizona Rattlers** arena football team (✆ 602/514-8383 or 602/379-7800; www.azrattlers.com) plays 50-yard indoor football at the America West Arena, 201 E. Jefferson St. Tickets are $5 to $44.

GOLF TOURNAMENTS It's not surprising that, with nearly 200 golf courses and ideal golfing weather throughout the fall, winter, and spring, the Valley of the Sun hosts three major PGA tournaments each year. Tickets for all three are available through Ticketmaster outlets (see above).

January's **Phoenix Open Golf Tournament** (✆ 602/870-4431; www.phoenixopen.com) is the largest. Held at the Tournament Players Club (TPC) of Scottsdale, it attracts more spectators than any other golf tournament in the world (more than 500,000 each year). The 18th hole has standing room for 40,000. Tickets start at $20.

Each March, the **PING Banner Health LPGA Tournament** (✆ 602/495-4653; www.standardregisterping.com), held at the Moon Valley Country Club, lures nearly 100 of the top women golfers from around the world. Daily tickets are $15; weekly tickets are $50.

The Tradition (✆ 480/595-4070; www.countrywidetradition. com), a Senior PGA Tour event held each April at the Desert Mountain course, has a loyal following of fans who would rather watch the likes of Jack Nicklaus and Chi Chi Rodriguez than see Tiger Woods win yet another tournament. Daily tickets are $10 to $20.

Now even amateurs can get in on some tournament action at the **Phoenix Amateur Golf Championship** (✆ 877/990-GOLF; www.phxamateur.com), held in late June (partly to prove that it's possible to play golf in the summer in Phoenix).

HOCKEY   The NHL's **Phoenix Coyotes** (℃ **888/255-PUCK** or 480/563-PUCK; www.phoenixcoyotes.com) play at the America West Arena. Tickets cost $9 to $175.

HORSE/GREYHOUND RACING   Turf Paradise, 1501 W. Bell Rd. (℃ **602/942-1101;** www.turfparadise.com), is Phoenix's horse-racing track. The season runs from late September to mid-May, with post time at 12:30pm. Admission ranges from $2 to $5.

The **Phoenix Greyhound Park,** 3801 E. Washington St. (℃ **602/273-7181;** www.phoenixgreyhoundpark.com), is a fully enclosed, air-conditioned facility offering seating in various grand-stands, lounges, and restaurants. There's racing throughout the year; tickets are $1.50 to $3.

RODEOS, POLO & HORSE SHOWS   Cowboys, cowgirls, and other horsey types will find plenty of four-legged critters going through their paces most weeks at **Westworld Equestrian Center,** 16601 N. Pima Rd., Scottsdale (℃ **480/312-6802**). With its 500 stables, 11 equestrian arenas, and a polo field, this 400-acre complex provides an amazing variety of entertainment and sporting events. There are rodeos, polo matches, horse shows, horseback rides, and horseback-riding instruction.

TENNIS TOURNAMENTS   Each March, top international men's tennis players compete at the **Franklin Templeton Tennis Classic** (℃ **480/922-0222;** www.scottsdaletennis.com), at the Fairmont Scottsdale Princess, 7575 E. Princess Dr., Scottsdale. Tickets run from $12 to $60 (tickets to later rounds are more expen-sive) and are available through Ticketmaster outlets (see above).

In late February, women's tennis players compete in the **State Farm Women's Tennis Classic** (℃ **480/778-9799;** www.scottsdale tennis.com), also held at the Fairmont Scottsdale Princess. Tickets cost $12 to $60 and are available through Ticketmaster (see above).

10 Day Spas

Ever since the first "lungers" showed up in the Phoenix area hoping to cure their tuberculosis, the desert has been a magnet for those looking to get healthy. In the first half of the 20th century, health spas were all the rage in Phoenix, and with the health-and-fitness trend continuing to gather steam, it comes as no surprise that spas are now once again immensely popular in the Valley of the Sun. In the past few years, several of the area's top resorts have added new full-service spas or expanded existing ones to cater to guests' increasing requests for services such as massages, body wraps, mud masks, and salt glows.

If you can't or don't want to spend the money to stay at a top resort and avail yourself of the spa, you may still be able to indulge. Most resorts open their spas to the public, and, for the cost of a body treatment or massage, you can spend the day at the spa, taking classes, working out in an exercise room, lounging by the pool, and otherwise living the life of the rich and famous. Barring this indulgence, you can slip into a day spa, of which there are many scattered around the valley, and take a stress-reduction break the way other people take a latte break.

If you want truly spectacular surroundings and bragging rights, head north to the **Golden Door Spa at the Boulders,** 34631 N. Tom Darlington Dr., Carefree (© **800/553-1717** or 480/488-9009; www.wyndham.com/luxury), which opened in 2001. This spa was one of three to open within a few months of one another, and though this one has the name recognition, it is, unfortunately, not the most impressive of the bunch. However, at 33,000 square feet and with 25 treatment spaces, it is certainly large. The turquoise wrap, the spa's signature treatment, is a real desert experience. Most 50-minute treatments cost around $115 to $120. Packages are $230 to $475.

Of the recent new arrivals in the valley, **Willow Stream–The Spa at Fairmont,** 7575 E. Princess Dr. (© **480/585-2732;** www.fairmont.com), is our favorite. Designed to conjure up images of the journey to Havasu Canyon, its highlights include a rooftop swimming pool and a large hot tub in a grotto below the pool. Because this is one of the largest spas in the valley, you'll stand a better chance of getting last-minute reservations here. Most 50-minute treatments cost $129 to $139. Packages range from $199 to $619; there are also several package options for couples. For $25, you can use the facilities for the day.

The **Spa at Gainey Village,** 7477 E. Doubletree Ranch Rd., Scottsdale (© **480/609-6980;** www.thespaatgaineyvillage.com), is a state-of-the-art spa and exercise facility near the Hyatt Regency Scottsdale. Although the health club seems to be the main draw, the spa offers a wide range of specialized treatments, including massage in a hydrotherapy tub, couples massages (complete with champagne and chocolate truffles), and just about anything else you can think of. With any 1-hour treatment (average price $85–$95), you can use the extensive exercise facilities or take a class. Packages range from $95 to $360.

Located high on the flanks of Mummy Mountain, the **Spa at Camelback Inn,** 5402 E. Lincoln Dr., Scottsdale (✆ **480/ 596-7040;** www.camelbackinn.com), is a great place to spend the day being pampered. For the cost of a single 1-hour treatment— between $100 and $115—you can use all the facilities. Among the treatments available are a para-joba body moisturizer that will leave your skin feeling like silk. Packages run from $165 to $310.

The **Centre for Well Being,** at the Phoenician, 6000 E. Camelback Rd., Scottsdale (✆ **800/843-2392** or 480/423-2452; www.thephoenician.com), is one of the valley's most prestigious spas. For as little as $110, you can get a 50-minute spa treatment (anything from a botanical hydrating wrap to Turkish body scrub) and then spend the day using the many facilities. Wellness consultations and even acupuncture are available. Packages range from $220 to $490.

The historic setting and convenient location of the **Arizona Biltmore Spa,** 24th Street and Missouri Avenue (✆ **602/381-7632** or 602/381-7683; www.arizonabiltmore.com), make this facility an excellent choice if you're spending time along the Camelback Corridor. The spa menu includes 80 different treatments, such as mud purification and desert body glow. If you have just one 50-minute treatment (priced at $95–$115), you can use all of the spa's facilities for the rest of the day. Packages cost $195 to $400.

The **Mist Spa,** at the Radisson Resort Scottsdale, 7171 N. Scottsdale Rd., Scottsdale (✆ **877/MIST-SPA** or 480/905-2882; www.themistspa.com), allows nonresort guests use of the facilities for $25 per day (the fee is waived with purchase of a spa treatment). The spa has a Japanese design, complete with Japanese-style massage rooms and a tranquil rock garden in a central courtyard. Treatments, which include the likes of collagen facials, Dead Sea mud wraps, and green-tea detoxifying wraps, cost $90 to $95. Packages range from $140 to $410.

7

Shopping

For the most part, shopping in the valley means malls. They're everywhere, and they're air-conditioned, which, we're sure you'll agree, makes shopping in the desert far more enjoyable when it's 110°F (43°C) outside.

Scottsdale and the Biltmore District of Phoenix (along Camelback Rd.) are the valley's main upscale shopping areas, with several high-end centers and malls. The various distinct shopping districts of downtown Scottsdale are among the few outdoor shopping areas in the valley and are home to hundreds of boutiques, galleries, jewelry stores, Native American crafts stores, and souvenir shops. The Western atmosphere of Old Town Scottsdale is partly real and partly a figment of the local merchants' imaginations, but nevertheless it's the most popular tourist shopping area in the valley. With dozens of galleries in the Main Street Arts and Antiques District and the nearby Marshall Way Contemporary Arts District, it also happens to be the heart of the valley's art market.

For locals, Scottsdale's shopping scene has been moving steadily northward, and in the past couple of years two new shopping centers—Kierland Commons and the Shops at Gainey Village—have been basking in the limelight.

Shopping hours are usually Monday through Saturday from 10am to 6pm and Sunday from noon to 5pm; malls usually stay open until 9pm Monday through Saturday.

1 Malls & Shopping Centers

Arizona Center   With its gardens and fountains, this modern downtown shopping center is both a peaceful oasis amid downtown's asphalt and a good place to shop for Arizona souvenirs if you happen to be in the area. However, it's not worth going out of your way for. It's also home to several nightclubs and Sam's Cafe, which serves Southwestern-style meals. Van Buren St. and Third St. © 602/ 949-4FUN. www.arizonacenter.com.

Biltmore Fashion Park   This open-air shopping plaza with garden courtyards is *the* place to be if shopping is your obsession. Storefronts bear the names of exclusive boutiques such as Gucci and Cartier. Saks Fifth Avenue and Macy's are the two anchors. There are also more than a dozen moderately priced restaurants here. E. Camelback Rd. and 24th St. (C) **602/955-1963.** www.shopbiltmore.com.

The Borgata of Scottsdale   Designed to resemble a medieval Italian village complete with turrets, stone walls, and ramparts, the Borgata is far and away the most architecturally interesting mall in the valley. It contains about 50 upscale boutiques, galleries, and restaurants. 6166 N. Scottsdale Rd. (C) **480/998-1822.** www.borgata.com.

El Pedregal Festival Marketplace   Located adjacent to the Boulders resort, 30 minutes north of Old Scottsdale, El Pedregal is the most self-consciously Southwestern shopping center in the valley, and it's worth the long drive out just to see the neo–Santa Fe architecture. The shops offer high-end merchandise, fashions, and art. The Heard Museum also has a branch here. 34505 N. Scottsdale Rd., Carefree. (C) **480/488-1072.** www.elpedregal.com.

Kierland Commons   The urban-village concept of a shopping center—narrow streets, sidewalks, and residences mixed in with retail space—has been taking off all over the country. Here in Scottsdale, the urban village has taken on Texas-size proportions, but despite the grand scale of this shopping center, it still has a great feel. You'll find Tommy Bahama, Ann Taylor Loft, Crate & Barrel, and even a few shops you may never have heard of before. 15210 N. Scottsdale Rd. (C) **480/951-1100.**

Scottsdale Fashion Square   Scottsdale has long been the valley's shopping mecca, and for years this huge mall has been the reason why. It now houses four major department stores—Nordstrom, Dillard's, Neiman Marcus, and Robinsons-May—and smaller stores such as Eddie Bauer, J. Crew, and Louis Vuitton. 7014–590 E. Camelback Rd. (at Scottsdale Rd.), Scottsdale. (C) **480/941-2140.** www.westcor.com.

The Shops at Gainey Village   This new upscale shopping center is much smaller than Kierland Commons farther up Scottsdale Road, but is no less impressive, especially after dark when blue lights illuminate the tall palm trees. In addition to several women's clothing stores, there are a couple of great restaurants. N. Scottsdale and Doubletree Ranch roads. (C) **480/998-1822.**

2 Goods A to Z

ANTIQUES & COLLECTIBLES

With more than 80 antiques shops and specialty stores, downtown Glendale (northwest of downtown Phoenix) is the valley's main antiques district. You'll find the greatest concentration of antiques stores just off Grand Avenue between 56th and 59th avenues. Five times a year, the **Phoenix Antique Market** (© 800/678-9987 or 602/943-1766; www.jackblack.com), Arizona's largest collectors' show, is held at the Arizona State Fairgrounds, 19th Avenue and McDowell Road. Shows are usually in January, February, May, September, and November.

Antiques Super-Mall   If you love browsing through packed antiques malls searching for your favorite collectibles, then this should be your first stop in the valley. It's one of the biggest antiques malls in the area, and within a block are two others: the **Antique Centre,** 2012 N. Scottsdale Rd. (© 480/675-9500), and the **Antique Trove,** 2020 N. Scottsdale Rd. (© 480/947-6074). 1900 N. Scottsdale Rd., Scottsdale. © 480/874-2900.

Arizona West Galleries   Nowhere else in Scottsdale will you find such an amazing collection of cowboy collectibles and Western antiques. There are antique saddles and chaps, old rifles and six-shooters, sheriffs' badges, spurs, and the like. 7149 E. Main St., Scottsdale. © 480/994-3752.

Bishop Gallery for Art & Antiques   This cramped shop is wonderfully eclectic, featuring everything from Asian antiques to unusual original art. Definitely worth a browse. 7164 Main St., Scottsdale. © 480/949-9062. www.Bishop-Gallery.com.

ART

In the Southwest, only Santa Fe is a more important art market than Scottsdale, and along the streets of Scottsdale's Main Street Arts and Antiques District and the Marshall Way Contemporary Arts District, you'll see dozens of galleries selling everything from monumental bronzes to contemporary art created from found objects. On Main Street, you'll find primarily cowboy art, both traditional and contemporary, while on North Marshall Way, you'll discover much more imaginative and daring contemporary art.

The annual **Celebration of Fine Art** (© 480/443-7695; www.celebrateart.com) takes place each year between mid-January and late March. Not only will you get to see the work of 100 artists, but on any given day, you'll also find dozens of the artists at work on the premises. Call for this year's location and hours of operation.

In addition to the galleries listed here, you'll usually find a huge tent full of art along Scottsdale Road in north Scottsdale.

Art One   This gallery specializes in works by art students and other area cutting-edge artists. The works here can be surprisingly good, and prices are very reasonable. 4120 N. Marshall Way, Scottsdale. 𝒞 480/946-5076. www.artonegallery.com.

gallerymateria   Representing emerging artists from the Americas, Asia, and Europe, this fascinating gallery focuses on contemporary fine crafts, including furniture, ceramics, and jewelry. 4222 N. Marshall Way, Scottsdale. 𝒞 480/949-1262. www.gallerymateria.com.

Hollywood Cowboy   If you believe that nothing says *cowboy* like an old Western movie, then be sure to check out the movie posters at this Scottsdale poster gallery. Old B Westerns are the specialty. 7077 E. Main St., Scottsdale. 𝒞 480/949-5646. www.hollywoodcowboy.com.

Lisa Sette Gallery   If you aren't a fan of cowboy or Native American art, don't despair. Instead, drop by this gallery, which represents international and local artists working in a wide mix of media. 4142 N. Marshall Way, Scottsdale. 𝒞 480/990-7342. www.lisasette gallery.com.

Meyer Gallery   This gallery is notable for its selection of Old West, landscape, and mood paintings by living Impressionists. Most interesting are the original paintings for the covers of Western pulp-fiction novels. 7173 E. Main St., Scottsdale. 𝒞 480/947-6372. www.meyer galleries.com.

Overland Gallery of Fine Art   Traditional Western and Russian Impressionist paintings form the backbone of this gallery's fine collection. These are museum-quality works (prices sometimes approach $100,000) and definitely worth a look. 7155 Main St., Scottsdale. 𝒞 480/947-1934.

Roberts Gallery   The feathered masks and sculptures of Virgil Walker are the highlights here, and if you have an appreciation for fine detail work, you'll likely be fascinated by these pieces. Walker's annual show is held on Thanksgiving weekend. El Pedregal Festival Marketplace, 34505 N. Scottsdale Rd., Carefree. 𝒞 480/488-1088.

Wilde Meyer Gallery   Brightly colored and playful are the watchwords at this gallery, which represents Linda Carter-Holman, a Southwestern favorite who does cowgirl-inspired paintings.

There's also a Wilde Meyer gallery at El Pedregal Festival Marketplace, Carefree (© 480/488-3200). 4142 N. Marshall Way, Scottsdale. © 480/945-2323.

BOOKS

Major chain bookstores in the area include **Borders,** at 2402 E. Camelback Rd., Phoenix (© **602/957-6660**), 699 S. Mill Ave., Tempe (© **480/921-8659**), and 4555 E. Cactus Rd., Paradise Valley (© **602/953-9699**); and **Barnes & Noble,** at 10235 N. Metro Parkway E., Phoenix (© **602/678-0088**), 4847 E. Ray Rd., Phoenix (© **480/940-7136**), and 10500 N. 90th St., Scottsdale (© **480/391-0048**).

The Poisoned Pen The store name and the police-style outline of a body on the floor should give you a clue as to what sort of bookstore this is. If you still haven't figured out that it specializes in mysteries, then maybe you should stick to other genres. 4014 N. Goldwater Blvd., Suite 101, Scottsdale. © **888/560-9919** or 480/947-2974. www.poisonedpen.com.

FASHION

Favorite mall destinations for upscale fashion include Biltmore Fashion Park, the Borgata of Scottsdale, El Pedregal Festival Marketplace, and Scottsdale Fashion Square. See "Malls & Shopping Centers," above, for details.

For cowboy and cowgirl attire, see "Western Wear," below.

Carole Dolighan Dolighan's hand-painted, hand-woven dresses, skirts, and blouses abound in rich colors. Each is unique. There's another Carole Dolighan store at El Pedregal Festival Marketplace, 34505 N. Scottsdale Rd., Carefree (© **480/488-4505**). At the Borgata, 6166 N. Scottsdale Rd., Scottsdale. © 480/922-0616.

Objects This eclectic shop carries hand-painted, wearable art that's both casual and dressy, along with unique artist-made jewelry, contemporary furnishings, and all kinds of delightful and unusual things. 8787 N. Scottsdale Rd., Scottsdale. © **480/994-4720**. www.objects gallery.com.

Uh Oh Uh Oh carries simple, tasteful, and oh-so-elegant (as well as Scottsdale hip) fashions, footwear, jewelry, and accessories. There are also stores at Kierland Commons, 15210 N. Scottsdale Rd., Scottsdale; and La Mirada, 8900 E. Pinnacle Peak Rd., Scottsdale. The phone number below works for all three stores. At Hilton Village, 6137 N. Scottsdale Rd., Scottsdale. © **480/991-1618**. www.uhohclothing.com.

GIFTS & SOUVENIRS

Bischoff's Shades of the West   This is a one-stop shop for all things Southwestern. From T-shirts to regional foodstuffs, this sprawling store has it all. It carries good selections of candles, wrought-iron cabinet hardware that will give your kitchen a Western look, and Mexican crafts. 7247 Main St., Scottsdale. ℭ **480/945-3289**. www.shadesofthewest.com.

A GOLF SHOP

In Celebration of Golf   Sort of a supermarket for golfers (with a touch of Disneyland thrown in), this amazing store sells everything from clubs and shoes to golf art and golf antiques. A golf simulation room allows you to test out new clubs. An old club-maker's workbench, complete with talking mannequin, makes a visit to this shop educational as well as fun. 7001 N. Scottsdale Rd., Suite 172, Scottsdale. ℭ **480/951-4444**. www.celebrategolf.com.

JEWELRY

Cornelis Hollander   Although this shop is much smaller and not nearly so dramatic as that of the nearby Jewelry by Gauthier, the designs are just as cutting edge. Whether you're looking for classic chic or trendy modern designs, you'll find plenty to interest you here. 4151 N. Marshall Way, Scottsdale. ℭ **480/423-5000**. www.CornelisHollander.com.

Jewelry by Gauthier   This elegant store sells the designs of the phenomenally talented Scott Gauthier. The stylishly modern pieces use precious stones and are miniature works of art. 4211 N. Marshall Way, Scottsdale. ℭ **888/411-3232** or 480/941-1707. www.jewelrybygauthier.com.

Molina Fine Jewelers   If you can spend as much on a necklace as you can on a Mercedes, then this is *the* place to shop for your baubles. Although you don't need an appointment, it's highly recommended. You'll then get personalized service as you peruse the Tiffany exclusives and high-end European jewelry. 3134 E. Camelback Rd. ℭ **800/257-2695** or 602/955-2055. www.molinafinejewelers.com.

NATIVE AMERICAN ARTS, CRAFTS & JEWELRY

Bischoff's at the Park   This museumlike store and gallery is affiliated with another Bischoff's right across the street (see above under "Gifts & Souvenirs"). This outpost carries higher-end jewelry, Western-style home furnishings and clothing, ceramics, sculptures, books and music with a regional theme, and contemporary paintings. 3925 N. Brown Ave., Scottsdale. ℭ **480/946-6155**. www.shadesofthewest.com.

Faust Gallery Fine American Indian Art Old Native American baskets and pottery, as well as old and new Navajo rugs, are the specialties at this interesting shop. It also sells Native American and Southwestern art, including ceramics, paintings, bronzes, and unusual sculptures. 7103 E. Main St., Scottsdale. ✆ 480/946-6345. www.faustgallery.com.

Gilbert Ortega Museum Gallery You'll find Gilbert Ortega shops all over the valley, but this is the biggest and best. As the name implies, there are museum displays throughout the store. Jewelry is the main attraction, but there are also baskets, sculptures, pottery, rugs, paintings, and kachina dolls. There's another Gilbert Ortega store nearby at 7237 E. Main St., Scottsdale (✆ **480/481-0788**). 3925 N. Scottsdale Rd. ✆ 480/990-1808.

Heard Museum Gift Shop The Heard Museum (p. 96) gift store has an astonishing collection of well-crafted and very expensive Native American jewelry, art, and crafts of all kinds. This is the best place in the valley to shop for Native American arts and crafts; you can be absolutely assured of the quality. Because the store doesn't have to charge sales tax, you'll save a bit of money. At the Heard Museum, 2301 N. Central Ave. ✆ 800/252-8344 or 602/252-8344. www.heard.org.

John C. Hill Antique Indian Art Not only does the store have one of the finest selections of Navajo rugs in the valley, including quite a few older rugs, but there are also kachina dolls, superb Navajo and Zuni silver-and-turquoise jewelry, baskets, and pottery. 6962 E. First Ave., Scottsdale. ✆ 480/946-2910.

Old Territorial Shop This is the oldest Indian arts-and-crafts store on Main Street and offers good values on jewelry, concha belts, kachinas, fetishes, pottery, and Navajo rugs. 7220 E. Main St., Scottsdale. ✆ 480/945-5432. www.oldterritorialshop.com.

OUTLET MALLS & DISCOUNT SHOPPING

Arizona Mills This huge mall in Tempe is on the cutting edge when it comes to shop-o-tainment. You'll find lots of name-brand outlets, a video arcade, a multiplex theater, and an IMAX theater. 5000 Arizona Mills Circle, Tempe. ✆ 480/491-9700. www.arizonamills.com. From I-10, take the Baseline Rd. east exit. From Ariz. 60, exit Priest Dr. south.

My Sister's Closet This is where the crème de la crème of Scottsdale's used clothing comes to be resold. You'll find such labels as Armani, Donna Karan, and Calvin Klein. Prices are pretty reasonable, too. Also at Town & Country shopping plaza, at 20th

Street and Camelback Road, Phoenix (© **602/954-6080**). At Lincoln Village, 6206 N. Scottsdale Rd. (near Trader Joe's), Scottsdale. © **480/443-4575**. www.mysisterscloset.com.

WESTERN WEAR

Az-Tex Hat Company   If you're looking to bring home a cowboy hat, this is a good place to get it. The small shop in Old Scottsdale offers custom shaping and fitting of both felt and woven hats. There's a second store at 15044 N. Cave Creek Rd., Phoenix (© **602/971-9090**). 3903 N. Scottsdale Rd., Scottsdale. © **800/972-2116** or 480/481-9900. www.aztexhats.com.

Out West   If the revival of 1950s cowboy fashions and interior decor has hit your nostalgia button, then you'll want to high-tail it up to this eclectic shop. All things Western are available, and the fashions are both beautiful and fun (although fancy and pricey). At El Pedregal Festival Marketplace, 34505 N. Scottsdale Rd., Carefree. © **480/488-0180**.

Saba's Western Stores   Since 1927, this store has been outfitting Scottsdale's cowboys and cowgirls, visiting dude ranchers, and anyone else who wants to adopt the look of the Wild West. Call for other locations around Phoenix. 7254 Main St., Scottsdale. © **480/949-7404**. www.sabaswesternwear.com.

Sheplers Western Wear   Although it isn't the largest Western-wear store in the valley, Sheplers is still sort of a department store of cowboy duds. If you can't find it here, it just ain't available in these parts. Other locations include 8979 E. Indian Bend Rd., Scottsdale (© **480/948-1933**); 2643 E. Broadway Rd., Mesa (© **480/827-8244**); and 2700 W. Baseline Rd., Tempe (© **602/438-7400**). 9201 N. 29th Ave. © **602/870-8085**. www.sheplers.com.

Stockman's Cowboy & Southwestern Wear   This is one of the oldest Western-wear businesses in the valley, although the store is now housed in a modern shopping plaza. You'll find swirly skirts, denim jackets, suede coats, and flashy cowboy shirts. Prices are reasonable and quality is high. 23587 N. Scottsdale Rd. (at Pinnacle Peak Rd.), Scottsdale. © **480/585-6142**.

8

Phoenix, Scottsdale & the Valley of the Sun After Dark

If you're looking for nightlife in the Valley of the Sun, you won't have to look hard, but you may have to drive quite a ways. Although much of the nightlife scene is centered on Old Scottsdale, Tempe's Mill Avenue, and downtown Phoenix, you'll find things going on all over.

The weekly *Phoenix New Times* tends to have the most comprehensive listings for clubs and concert halls. The *Rep Entertainment Guide,* in the Thursday edition of the *Arizona Republic* (and also distributed free of charge from designated newspaper boxes on sidewalks around the valley) also lists upcoming events and performances. *Get Out,* published by the *Tribune,* is another tabloid-format arts-and-entertainment publication that is available free around Scottsdale and Tempe. Other publications to check for abbreviated listings are *Valley Guide Quarterly, Key to the Valley, Where Phoenix/Scottsdale,* and *Quick Guide Arizona,* all of which are free and can usually be found at hotels and resorts.

Tickets to many concerts, theater performances, and sporting events are available through **Ticketmaster** (© **480/784-4444;** www.ticketmaster.com), which has outlets at Wherehouse Records, Tower Records, and Robinsons-May department stores.

1 The Club & Music Scene

In **downtown Scottsdale,** you'll find an eclectic array of clubs in the neighborhoods surrounding the corner of Camelback Road and Scottsdale Road (especially along Stetson Dr., which is divided into two sections east and west of Scottsdale Rd.). This is where the wealthy (and the wannabes) come to party, and you'll see lots of limos pulling up in front of the hot spots of the moment (currently Axis/Radius, Sanctuary, Six, and the Velvet Room).

Another place to wander around until you hear your favorite type of music is **Mill Avenue** in Tempe. Because Tempe is a college town, there are plenty of clubs and bars on this short stretch of road.

With a sports bar, several other bars and clubs, a multiplex theater, and several restaurants, downtown Phoenix's **Arizona Center** is a veritable entertainment mecca. Within a few blocks of this complex are Symphony Hall, the Herberger Theater Center, and several sports bars. Much of the action revolves around games and concerts at the America West Arena and Bank One Ballpark (BOB).

To find out what's hot on the club scene, grab a copy of the *New Times*. Many dance clubs in the Phoenix area are open only on weekends, so be sure to check what night the doors will be open. Bars and clubs are allowed to serve alcohol until 1am.

COMEDY & CABARET

The Tempe Improv   With the best of the national comedy circuit harassing the crowds and rattling off one-liners, the Improv is the valley's most popular comedy club. Dinner is served and reservations are advised. 930 E. University Dr., Tempe. ℂ 480/921-9877. www.improvclubs.com. Cover $12–$15, plus 2-item minimum.

COUNTRY MUSIC

Handlebar-J   We're not saying that this Scottsdale landmark is a genuine cowboy bar, but cowpokes do make this one of their stops when they come in from the ranch. You'll hear live git-down two-steppin' nightly; free dance lessons are given Wednesday, Thursday, and Sunday. 7116 E. Becker Lane, Scottsdale. ℂ 480/948-0110. No cover to $4.

Rusty Spur Saloon   A small and rowdy drinkin'-and-dancin' place frequented by tourists, this bar is a lot of fun, with peanut shells all over the floor, dollar bills stapled to the walls, and the occasional live act in the afternoon or evening. 7245 E. Main St., Old Scottsdale. ℂ 480/941-2628.

DANCE CLUBS & DISCOS

Axis/Radius   If you're looking to do a bit of celebrity-spotting, Axis is the place. Currently Scottsdale's hottest dance club and liveliest singles scene, this two-story glass box is a boldly contemporary space with an awesome sound system. 7340 E. Indian Plaza (2 blocks east of Scottsdale Rd. and 1 block south of Camelback Rd.), Scottsdale. ℂ 480/970-1112. Cover $5–$10.

Buzz Original Funbar   In Scottsdale, folks like to think big. Buzz is no exception, boasting three different theme areas: the Rat Pack

Lounge, the Rhino Room (with a zebra-striped dance floor), and a rooftop patio. Clientele is primarily of the barely legal persuasion. 10345 N. Scottsdale Rd. (at Shea Blvd.). ✆ **480/991-FUNN.** No cover to $10.

Club Rio Popular primarily with students from ASU, which is just across the Tempe Town Lake, this club has a dance floor big enough for football practice. Music is primarily Top 40, alternative, and retro, and there are plenty of live shows. 430 N. Scottsdale Rd., Tempe. ✆ **480/894-0533.** www.clubrio.com. No cover to $10.

Pepin Friday and Saturday, a DJ plays Latin dance music from 10pm on at this small Spanish restaurant located in the Scottsdale Mall. Thursday through Saturday evenings, there are also live flamenco performances. 7363 Scottsdale Mall, Scottsdale. ✆ **480/990-9026.** Cover $8.

Phoenix Live! at Arizona Center Located on the second floor of the Arizona Center shopping center in downtown Phoenix, this trio of clubs (a piano bar, a dance club, and a sports bar) provides enough options to keep almost any group of barhoppers happy. 455 N. Third St. ✆ **602/252-2502.** No cover to $5.

Sanctuary Sanctuary, one of the hottest clubs in downtown Scottsdale, has raised the bar for high-end dance clubs. As with other area megaclubs, there are different theme rooms, including a Moroccan room. Lots of laser lights and great martinis. Open Wednesday, Friday, and Saturday nights only. 7340 E. Shoeman Lane, Scottsdale. ✆ **480/970-5000.** www.sanctuaryclub.com. Cover $3–$7 for women, $5–$10 for men.

JAZZ & BLUES

Char's Has the Blues Yes, indeed, Char's does have those mean-and-dirty, low-down blues, and if you want them too, this is where you head in Phoenix. All of the best blues brothers and sisters from around the city and around the country make the scene. 4631 N. Seventh Ave., 4 blocks south of Camelback Rd. ✆ **602/230-0205.** www.charshas theblues.com. No cover to $10.

The Famous Door Martinis and cigars are de rigueur with the affluent 20- and 30-something crowd here. With a jazz combo wedged into the corner and a pall of smoke hanging in the air, this place manages to pull it off. 7419 Indian Plaza, Scottsdale. ✆ **480/ 970-1945.** www.thefamousdoor.com.

A League of Our Own The dinner club/jazz club is a concept that is taking off in a big way here in the valley, and this out-of-the-way spot is at the forefront. Tuesday through Sunday, there's live jazz by some of the best local musicians. At Uptown Plaza, Central Ave. and Camelback Rd. © 602/265-2354. www.aleagueofourown.net. $25 per person minimum after 10pm if you want a table near the stage; otherwise, no cover.

The Rhythm Room This blues club, long the valley's most popular, books quite a few national acts as well as the best of the local scene, and has a dance floor if you want to move to the beat. 1019 E. Indian School Rd. © 602/265-4842. www.rhythmroom.com. No cover to $15.

Velvet Room Supper Club Here's another Scottsdale nightclub affecting a retro New York character: that of a classic supper club. Although this place is small, it's got loads of atmosphere and live music nightly. When national acts are playing, there are two shows nightly. 7111 E. Fifth Ave., Scottsdale. © 480/941-6000. www.thevelvetroom. com. No cover to $20.

ROCK & ALTERNATIVE MUSIC

The Bash on Ash If it appeals to college students, you'll hear it on stage at Tempe's top live-music club. Currently salsa and swing each get their own night of the week, while heavy metal, reggae, and alternative get equal time, too. 230 W. Fifth St., Tempe. © 480/966-8200. www.bashonash.com. Cover $7–$20.

Cajun House The interior of this cavernous live music venue and dance club is done up as a New Orleans street scene, with doors opening into various bars, dining rooms, and lounges. Rock, blues, jazz, and alternative are all on the docket. Fun and worth checking out. 7117 E. Third Ave., Scottsdale. © 480/945-5150. www.cajunhouse.com. Cover $7 and up.

2 The Bar, Lounge & Pub Scene

AZ88 Across the park from the Scottsdale Center for the Arts, this sophisticated bar/restaurant has a cool ambience that's just right for a cocktail before or after a performance. There's also a great patio area. 7353 Scottsdale Mall, Scottsdale. © 480/994-5576.

Bandersnatch Brew Pub With good house brews and a big patio in back, Bandersnatch is a favorite of those unusual ASU students who prefer quality to quantity when it's beer-drinking time. There's live Irish music on Wednesday. 125 E. Fifth St., Tempe. © 480/966-4438. www.bandersnatchpub.com.

Bar Bianco Located downtown on Heritage Square, this little wine bar is in a restored historic home and is affiliated with Pizzeria

Bianco, the tiny and ever-popular designer pizza place right next door. With cozy furnishings and candles, this is far and away the most romantic bar downtown. 609 E. Adams St. ✆ 602/528-3699.

Durant's In business for decades, Durant's has long been downtown Phoenix's favorite after-work watering hole with the old guard and has caught on with the young martini-drinking crowd as well. Through wine coolers, light beers, and microbrews, Durant's has remained true to the martini and other classic cocktails. 2611 N. Central Ave. ✆ 602/264-5967. www.durantsfinefoods.com.

Four Peaks Brewing Company Consistently voted the best brewpub in Phoenix, this Tempe establishment brews good beers and serves decent pub grub. A favorite of ASU students. 1340 E. Eighth St., Tempe. ✆ 480/303-9967. www.fourpeaks.com.

Hyatt Regency Scottsdale Lobby Bar The open-air lounge just below the main lobby of this posh Scottsdale resort sets a romantic stage for nightly live music (often Spanish-influenced guitar or flamenco music). Wood fires burn in patio fire pits, and the terraced gardens offer plenty of dark spots for a bit of romance. 7500 E. Doubletree Ranch Rd., Scottsdale. ✆ 480/991-3388.

Kazimierz World Wine Bar A spacious speakeasy crossed with a wine bar, this unmarked place, associated with the nearby Cowboy Ciao restaurant, offers the same wide selection of wines available at the restaurant. 7137 E. Stetson Dr., Scottsdale. ✆ 480/946-3004.

Postino This immensely popular wine bar is located in the heart of the Arcadia neighborhood south of Camelback Road. Casual yet stylish, the bar has garage-style doors that can roll up to open onto the patio. Choose from a great selection of wines by the glass and a limited menu of European-inspired appetizers. 3939 E. Campbell Ave. ✆ 602/852-3939.

The Squaw Peak Bar Can't afford the lap of luxury? For the cost of a couple of drinks, you can sink into a seat here at the Biltmore's main lounge and watch the sunset test its color palette on Squaw Peak. Alternatively, you can slide into a seat near the piano and let the waves of mellow jazz wash over you. At the Arizona Biltmore Resort & Spa, 2400 E. Missouri Ave. ✆ 602/955-6600.

T. Cook's If you aren't planning on having dinner at this opulent restaurant, at least stop by for a cocktail in the bar. With its mix of Spanish-colonial and 1950s tropical furnishings, this is as romantic a lounge as you'll find anywhere in the valley. You can also snuggle with your sweetie out on the patio by the fireplace. At the Royal Palms Hotel and Casitas, 5200 E. Camelback Rd. ✆ **602/808-0766.**

Thirsty Camel   Whether you've already made your millions or are still working your way up the corporate ladder, you owe it to yourself to spend a little time surrounded by luxury. You may never drink in more ostentatious surroundings than here at Charles Keating's Xanadu. The view's pretty good, too. At the Phoenician, 6000 E. Camelback Rd. ✆ **480/941-8200,** ext. 3558.

COCKTAILS WITH A VIEW

The restaurants **Different Pointe of View** (p. 90), at the Pointe Hilton Tapatio Cliffs Resort; **Rustler's Rooste** (p. 91), at the Pointe South Mountain Resort; and **Top of the Rock** (p. 90), at The Buttes have lounges, where, for the price of a drink, you can sit back and ogle a crimson sunset and the purple mountains' majesty.

SPORTS BARS

Alice Cooper'stown   Sports and rock mix it up at this downtown restaurant/bar run by, you guessed it, Alice Cooper. The Bank One Ballpark is only a block away. See p. 120. 101 E. Jackson St. ✆ **602/253-7337.** Most nights no cover; special shows up to $25.

Majerle's Sports Grill   If you're a Phoenix Suns fan, you won't want to miss this sports bar located only a couple of blocks from the America West Arena, where the Suns play. Suns memorabilia covers the walls. 24 N. Second St. ✆ **602/253-9004.**

McDuffy's   With 70 TVs and two dozen beers on tap, this is a favorite of Sun Devils fans. 230 W. Fifth St. (a block off Mill Ave.), Tempe. ✆ **480/966-5600.**

Phoenix Live/America's Original Sports Bar   Located in the Arizona Center, this enormous sports bar has a huge deck, innumerable TVs, and even a Phoenix Sports Hall of Fame. 455 N. Third St. ✆ **602/252-2502.** No cover to $5.

GAY & LESBIAN BARS & CLUBS

Ain't Nobody's Bizness   Located in a small shopping plaza, this is the city's most popular lesbian bar, with pool tables and a smoke-free lounge. On weekends, the dance floor is usually packed. 3031 E. Indian School Rd. ✆ **602/224-9977.**

Amsterdam   This downtown Phoenix bar may not look like much from the outside, but inside you'll find a classy spot that's known for its great martinis. Mondays feature martini specials and

Tuesdays bring female impersonators. Other nights, there's live music or DJ dance music. 718 N. Central Ave. ✆ **602/258-6122.**

3 The Performing Arts

Although downtown Phoenix claims the valley's greatest concentration of performance halls, including Symphony Hall, the Orpheum Theatre, and the Herberger Theater Center, there are major performing-arts venues scattered across the valley. No matter where you're staying, you're likely to find performances being held nearby.

Calling these many valley venues home are such major companies as the Phoenix Symphony, Scottsdale Symphony Orchestra, Arizona Opera Company, Ballet Arizona, Center Dance Ensemble, Actors Theatre of Phoenix, and Arizona Theatre Company. Adding to the performances held by these companies are the wide variety of touring companies that make stops here year-round.

While you'll find box-office phone numbers listed below, you can also purchase most performing-arts tickets through **Ticketmaster** (✆ **480/784-4444;** www.ticketmaster.com). For sold-out shows, check with your hotel concierge, or try **Western States Ticket Service** (✆ **602/254-3300;** www.wstickets.com) or **Tickets Unlimited** (✆ **800/289-8497** or 602/840-2340; www.ticketsunlimitedinc.com).

MAJOR PERFORMING-ARTS CENTERS

The **Dodge Theatre,** 400 W. Washington St. (✆ **602/379-2888;** www.dodgetheatre.com), which opened in 2002, is Phoenix's newest performance hall, seating from 2,000 to 5,000 people. It immediately began booking top names in entertainment (Jerry Seinfeld, Robin Williams, Harry Connick, Jr.) as well as Broadway shows and international touring companies. There are plans to add boxing matches to the calendar.

Phoenix's premier performance venue is **Symphony Hall,** 225 E. Adams St. (✆ **602/262-7272**), home to the Phoenix Symphony and the Arizona Opera Company. It also hosts touring Broadway shows and various other concerts and theatrical productions.

The **Orpheum Theatre,** 203 W. Adams St. (✆ **602/262-7272**), is the most elegant hall in the valley.

The Frank Lloyd Wright–designed **Grady Gammage Memorial Auditorium,** Mill Avenue and Apache Boulevard, Tempe (✆ **480/ 965-3434;** www.asu.edu), on ASU campus, is massive and graceful. This 3,000-seat hall hosts everything from barbershop quartets to touring Broadway shows.

The **Scottsdale Center for the Arts,** 7380 E. Second St., Scottsdale (© **480/994-ARTS;** www.scottsdalearts.org), hosts a variety of performances, ranging from alternative dance to classical music. This center seems to get the best of the touring performers.

In Scottsdale, ASU's **Kerr Cultural Center,** 6110 N. Scottsdale Rd. (© **480/965-5377;** www.asukerr.com), is a tiny venue in a historic home that offers up an eclectic season of music from around the world.

OUTDOOR VENUES & SERIES

The city's top outdoor venue is the **Cricket Pavilion,** a half mile north of I-10 between 79th and 83rd avenues (© **602/254-7200;** http://cricket-pavilion.com). This 20,000-seat amphitheater is open year-round and hosts everything from Broadway musicals to rock concerts.

The **Mesa Amphitheater,** at University Drive and Center Road, Mesa (© **480/644-2560**), is a much smaller amphitheater that holds a wide variety of concerts in spring and summer, and occasionally other times of year as well.

Throughout the year, the **Scottsdale Center for the Arts,** 7380 E. Second St., Scottsdale (© **480/994-ARTS;** www.scottsdale arts.org), stages outdoor performances in the adjacent Scottsdale Amphitheater on the Scottsdale Civic Center Mall. The Sunday A'fair series runs from October to April, with free concerts from noon to 4:30pm on selected Sundays of each month. Performances range from acoustic blues to zydeco.

Two perennial favorites of valley residents take place in particularly attractive surroundings. The Music in the Garden concerts at the **Desert Botanical Garden,** 1201 N. Galvin Pkwy., in Papago Park (© **480/941-1225;** www.dbg.org), are held on Sunday between September and March. The season always includes an eclectic array of musical styles. Tickets are $14 and include admission to the gardens. Sunday brunch is served for an additional charge. Up on the north side of the valley, in Carefree, **El Pedregal Festival Marketplace** (© **480/488-1072;** www.elpedregal.com) stages jazz, blues, and rock concerts on Thursday evenings in May, June, and July. Tickets are $10. Other times of year, there are also Sunday-afternoon concerts held at El Pedregal.

Outdoor concerts are also held at various parks and plazas around the valley during the warmer months. Check local papers for listings.

CLASSICAL MUSIC, OPERA & DANCE

The **Phoenix Symphony** (© **800/776-9080** or 602/495-1999; www.phoenixsymphony.org), the Southwest's leading symphony orchestra, performs at Symphony Hall (tickets run $18–$46), while the **Scottsdale Symphony Orchestra** (© **480/945-8071;** www.scotsymph.org) performs at the Scottsdale Center for the Arts (tickets go for $17–$20).

Opera buffs may want to see what the **Arizona Opera Company** (© **602/266-7464;** www.azopera.com) has scheduled. This company stages up to five operas, both familiar and more obscure, and splits its time between Phoenix and Tucson. Tickets cost $25 to $72. Performances are held at Symphony Hall.

Ballet Arizona (© **602/381-1096;** www.balletarizona.org) performs at Symphony Hall and the Orpheum and stages both classical and contemporary ballets; tickets run $15 to $42. The **Center Dance Ensemble** (© **602/252-8497;** www.centerdance.com), the city's contemporary dance company, stages several productions a year at the Herberger Theater Center. Tickets cost $18. Between September and March, **Southwest Arts & Entertainment** (© **602/482-6410**) brings acclaimed dance companies and music acts from around the world to Phoenix, with performances staged primarily at the Orpheum. Ticket prices range from $18 to $45.

THEATER

With nearly a dozen professional companies and the same number of nonprofessional companies taking to the boards year-round, there is always some play being staged somewhere in the valley.

The **Herberger Theater Center,** 222 E. Monroe St. (© **602/252-8497;** www.herbergertheater.org), which is located downtown, is the city's main venue for live theater. Its two Broadway-style theaters together host hundreds of performances each year, including productions by the **Actors Theatre of Phoenix (ATP)** and the **Arizona Theatre Company (ATC).** ATP (© **602/253-6701;** www.atphx.org) tends to stage smaller, lesser-known off-Broadway–type works, with musicals, dramas, and comedies equally represented; tickets go for $23 to $40. The annual production of *A Christmas Carol* is always a big hit. ATC (© **602/256-6899;** www.actorstheatrePHX.org) is the state theater company of Arizona and splits its performances between Phoenix and Tucson. Founded in 1967, it's the major force on the Arizona thespian scene. Productions range from world premieres to recent Tony award–winners to classics. Tickets run $25 to $48.

The **Phoenix Theatre,** 100 E. McDowell Rd. (✆ **602/ 254-2151**), has been around for almost 80 years and stages a wide variety of productions; tickets are $25 to $32. If your interest lies in Broadway plays, see what the **Broadway in Arizona Series** (✆ **480/ 965-3434;** www.broadwayacrossamerica.com/tempe) has scheduled. The series, focusing mostly on comedies and musicals, is held at the Gammage Auditorium in Tempe; tickets cost about $22 to $60. The **Theater League** (✆ **602/952-2881;** www.theaterleague.com) is another series that brings in Broadway musicals. Performances are held in the Orpheum Theatre, and tickets range from $34 to $40.

Scottsdale's small **Stagebrush Theatre,** 7020 E. Second St. (✆ **480/990-7405;** www.stagebrush.com), is a community theater that features tried-and-true comedies and musicals (plus children's theater), with the occasional drama thrown in. Tickets are about $10 for children's theater performances and $18 to $20 for other productions. For more daring new works and children's theater, check the schedule of **PlayWright's Theatre** (✆ **602/253-5151**), which stages its performances at various venues around the valley. Tickets are under $20. The **Arizona Jewish Theatre Co.** (✆ **602/ 264-0402;** www.azjewishtheatre.org), which stages plays by Jewish playwrights and with Jewish themes, performs at Playhouse on the Park, in the Viad Corporate Center, 1850 N. Central Ave. (at Palm Lane). Tickets range from $25 to $27.

4 Casinos

Casino Arizona at Salt River   The two casinos that make up this complex are the newest and most conveniently located casinos in the area. They have plenty of slot machines, cards, and other games of chance. They're not as impressive as the advertising campaign would have you believe, but they do stay packed. U.S. 101 and Indian Bend Rd., and U.S. 101 and McKellips Rd. ✆ 480/850-7777.

Fort McDowell Casino   Located about 45 minutes northeast of Scottsdale, this Indian casino is the oldest in the state, offering slot machines, video-poker games, and free shuttles from locations around the valley. On Fort McDowell Rd. off Ariz. 87, 2 miles northeast of Shea Blvd., Fountain Hills. ✆ 800/THE-FORT.

Harrah's Phoenix Ak-Chin Casino   This establishment on the Ak-Chin Indian Reservation features lots of slot machines, video poker, a card room, keno, and bingo. 15406 Maricopa Rd., Maricopa. ✆ 800/427-7247. Take Exit 164 (Queen Creek Rd.) off I-10, turn right, and drive 17 miles to the town of Maricopa.

9

Side Trips from Phoenix & Scottsdale

1 The Apache Trail ★★

There isn't a whole lot of desert or history left in Phoenix, but only an hour's drive to the east you'll find quite a bit of both. The Apache Trail, a narrow, winding, partially gravel road that snakes its way around the north side of the Superstition Mountains, offers some of the most scenic desert driving in central Arizona. Along the way are ghost towns and legends, saguaros and century plants, ancient ruins and artificial lakes. You could easily spend a couple of days traveling this route, though most people make it a day trip. Pick and choose the stops that appeal to you, and be sure to get an early start.

If you'd rather leave the driving to someone else, consider **Apache Trail Tours** (© 480/982-7661; www.apachetrailtours.com), which offers four-wheel-drive tours of different lengths ($75–$145), as well as hiking tours into the Superstition Mountains.

To start this drive, head east on U.S. 60 to the town of Apache Junction, and then go north on Ariz. 88. About 4 miles out of town, you'll come to **Goldfield Ghost Town,** a reconstructed gold-mining town (p.105). Leave yourself plenty of time if you plan to stop here.

Not far from Goldfield is **Lost Dutchman State Park** (© 480/982-4485), where you can hike into the rugged Superstition Mountains and see what the region's gold seekers were up against. Springtime wildflower displays here can be absolutely gorgeous. Park admission is $5 per vehicle; a campground charges $10 per site.

Continuing northeast, you'll reach **Canyon Lake,** set in a deep canyon flanked by colorful cliffs and rugged rock formations. It's the first of three reservoirs you'll pass on this drive. The three lakes provide much of Phoenix's drinking water. Here at Canyon Lake, you can go for a swim at the Acacia Picnic Area or the nearby Boulder Picnic Area, which is in a pretty side cove. You can also take a cruise

on the *Dolly* steamboat (© 480/827-9144; www.dollysteam boat.com). A 90-minute jaunt on this reproduction paddle wheeler costs $15 for adults and $8.50 for children 6 to 12. Dinner cruises are also available, and there's a lakeside restaurant at the boat landing. But if you're at all hungry, try to hold out for nearby **Tortilla Flat** (© 480/984-1776; www.tortillaflataz.com), an old stagecoach stop with a restaurant, saloon, and general store. Don't miss the prickly-pear ice cream (guaranteed spineless).

A few miles past Tortilla Flat, the pavement ends and the truly spectacular desert scenery begins. Among the rocky ridges, arroyos, and canyons of this stretch of road, you'll see saguaro cacti and century plants (a type of agave that dies after sending up its flower stalk, which can reach heights of 15 ft.). Next, you'll come to **Apache Lake,** which is not nearly as spectacular a setting as Canyon Lake, though it does have the **Apache Lake Marina and Resort** (© 928/467-2511; www.apachelake.com), with a motel, restaurant, general store, and campground. If you're inclined to turn this drive into an overnight trip, this would be a good place to spend the night. Room rates are $60 to $85; boat rentals are available.

Shortly before reaching pavement again, you'll see **Theodore Roosevelt Dam.** This dam, built in 1911, forms Roosevelt Lake and is the largest masonry dam in the world. However, a face-lift a few years ago hid the original masonry construction; it now looks much like any other concrete dam in the state.

Continuing on Ariz. 88, you'll come to **Tonto National Monument** ⚘ (✆ 520/467-2241; www.nps.gov/tont), which preserves some of the southernmost cliff dwellings in Arizona. These pueblos were occupied between about 1300 and 1450 by the Salado people and are some of the few remaining traces of this tribe, which once cultivated lands now flooded by Roosevelt Lake. The lower ruins are a half mile up a steep trail from the visitor center, while getting to the upper ruins requires a 3-mile round-trip hike. The lower ruins are open daily year-round; the upper ruins are open November through April on guided tours. Tour reservations are required (reserve at least 2 weeks in advance). The park is open daily from 8am to 5pm (you must begin the lower ruin trail by 4pm); admission is $3.

Keep going on Ariz. 88 to the copper-mining town of **Globe.** Although you can't see the mines themselves, the tailings (remains of rock removed from the copper ore) can be seen piled high all around the town. Be sure to visit **Besh-Ba-Gowah Archaeological Park** ⚘ (✆ 928/425-0320), on the eastern outskirts of town. This Salado Indian pueblo site has been partially reconstructed, and several rooms are set up to reflect the way they might have looked when they were first occupied about 700 years ago. For this reason, they're among the most fascinating ruins in the state. Open daily from 9am to 5pm; admission is $3 for adults, $2 for seniors, and free for children 12 and under. To get here, head out of Globe on South Broad Street to Jesse Hayes Road.

From Globe, head west on U.S. 60. Three miles west of Superior, you'll come to **Boyce Thompson Arboretum** ⚘⚘, 37615 U.S. 60 (✆ 520/689-2811; http://arboretum.ag.arizona.edu), dedicated to researching and propagating desert plants. This was the nation's first botanical garden established in the desert, and is set in two small but rugged canyons. From the impressive cactus gardens, you can gaze up at sun-baked cliffs before ducking into a forest of eucalyptus trees along the stream that runs through the arboretum. As you hike the miles of nature trails, watch for the two bizarre boojum trees. The arboretum is open daily from 8am to 5pm; admission is $6 for adults and $3 for children 5 to 12.

If you're looking for a place to eat, stop in at **Gold Canyon Golf Resort,** 6100 S. Kings Ranch Rd., Gold Canyon (© **480/982-9090**), which has a good formal dining room and a more casual bar and grill.

2 Southeast of Phoenix (En Route to Tucson)

Driving southeast from Phoenix for about 60 miles will bring you to the Florence and Casa Grande area, where you can learn about Indian cultures both past and present and view the greatest concentration of historic adobe buildings in Arizona. To reach Florence, drive south on I-10 to Exit 185 (Ariz. 387) and head east. If you're continuing south toward Tucson from Florence, we suggest taking the scenic **Pinal Pioneer Parkway** (Ariz. 79), which was the old highway between Phoenix and Tucson before the interstate was built. Along the way, you'll see signs identifying desert plants and a memorial to silent-film star Tom Mix, who died in a car crash here in 1940.

WHAT TO SEE & DO IN FLORENCE

Florence, which is home to a large state prison, may at first glance seem to have little to recommend it, but closer inspection turns up nearly 140 buildings on the National Register of Historic Places. The majority of these buildings were constructed of adobe and originally built in the Sonoran style, a style influenced by Spanish architectural ideas. Most buildings were altered over the years and now display aspects of various architectural styles popular during territorial days in Arizona. The current county courthouse, built in 1891, presents one of the oddest mixes of styles. The annual **Florence Historic Tour,** which takes place in early February, guides the public through 16 historic buildings. Tickets are $10 for adults ($8 in advance) and $5 for children ($3 in advance). To find out more about the tour and the town's many historic buildings, stop in at the **Florence Visitor Center,** 291 N. Bailey St. (© **800/437-9433** or 520/868-9433; www.florenceaz.org), in a historic 1891 bakery in the center of town.

McFarland State Historic Park   This historic park consists of the former Pinal County Courthouse, built in 1878. Inside the old adobe building, you'll see some rooms that re-create the days when this was the courthouse; other rooms are furnished from the days when this was a hospital. Exhibits focus on local lynchings and Florence's World War II POW camp.

Main and Ruggles sts. © 520/868-5216. www.pr.state.az.us. Suggested donation $2. Thurs–Mon 8am–5pm. Closed Christmas.

Pinal County Historical Museum Before touring the town, stop in at this small museum to orient yourself and learn more about the history of the area. You can blame the presence of the prison for the macabre exhibit of hanging nooses and a gas-chamber chair. There's also a collection of Tom Mix memorabilia.

715 S. Main St. ℂ 520/868-4382. Admission by donation. Tues–Sat 11am–4pm; Sun noon–4pm. Closed mid-July to Aug.

ATTRACTIONS ALONG THE WAY

There are a couple of **factory-outlet shopping malls** in the town of Casa Grande, at exits 194 and 198 off I-10. They are only a short distance out of your way to the south if you're headed back to Phoenix.

Casa Grande Ruins National Monument ★★ Located outside the town of Coolidge not far from Florence, this national monument preserves one of the most unusual Indian ruins in the state. In Spanish, *casa grande* means "big house," and that's exactly what you'll find. In this instance, the big house is the ruin of an earth-walled structure built 650 years ago by the Hohokam people. It is speculated that the building was once some sort of astronomical observatory, but this is not known for certain. Whatever the original purpose of the building, today it provides a glimpse of a style of ancient architecture rarely seen. Rather than using adobe bricks or stones, the people who built this structure used layers of hard-packed soil, which have survived the ravages of the weather and still stand in silent testament to the long-ago architectural endeavors of Hohokam. The Hohokam began farming the valleys of the Gila and Salt rivers about 1,500 years ago, and eventually built an extensive network of irrigation canals for watering their fields. By the middle of the 15th century, the Hohokam had abandoned both their canals and their villages and disappeared without a trace.

Ariz. 87, 1 mile north of Coolidge. ℂ 520/723-3172. www.nps.gov/cagr. Admission $3. Daily 8am–5pm. Closed Christmas.

Picacho Peak State Park ★★ If you're heading to Tucson by way of I-10, and it isn't too hot outside, consider a stop at this state park, 35 miles northwest of Tucson at Exit 219. Picacho Peak, a wizard's cap of rock rising 1,500 feet above the desert, is a visual landmark for miles around. Hiking trails lead around the lower slopes of the peak and up to the summit; these trails are especially popular in spring, when the wildflowers bloom (the park is known as one of the best places in Arizona to see wildflowers). In addition to its natural beauty, Picacho Peak was the site of the only Civil War battle to take place in the state. Each March, Civil War reenactments are staged here. Campsites in the park cost $10 to $17.

Exit 219 off I-10. ℭ **520/466-3183**. www.pr.state.az.us. Admission $5 per car.

3 En Route to Northern Arizona

If your idea of a great afternoon is searching out deals at factory-outlet stores, then you'll be in heaven at the **Outlets at Anthem,** 4250 W. Anthem Way (ℭ **888/482-5834** or 623/465-9500; www.outletsanthem.com). Among the offerings are Ann Taylor, Geoffrey Beene, Polo Ralph Lauren, and Levi's. Take Exit 229 (Anthem Way) off I-17.

Some 13 miles farther north is the town of Rock Springs, which is barely a wide spot in the road and is easily missed by drivers roaring up and down I-17. However, if you're a fan of pies, then do *not* miss Exit 242. Here you'll find the **Rock Springs Cafe** (ℭ **623/374-5794**), in business since 1920. Although this aging, nondescript building looks like the sort of place that would best be avoided, the packed parking lot says different. Why so popular? It's not the coffee or the "hogs in heat" barbecue or even the Bradshaw Mountain oysters. No, what keeps this place packed are Penny's pies, the most famous in Arizona. Each year, nearly 40,000 pies are sold here! If one slice isn't enough, order a whole pie to go.

If you appreciate innovative architecture, don't miss the Cordes Junction exit (Exit 262) off I-17. Here, you'll find **Arcosanti** (ℭ **520/632-7135** or 602/254-5309; www.arcosanti.org), Italian architect Paolo Soleri's vision of the future—a "city" that merges architecture and ecology. Soleri, who came to Arizona to study with Frank Lloyd Wright at Taliesin West, envisions a compact, energy-efficient city that disturbs the natural landscape as little as possible—and that's just what's rising out of the desert here at Arcosanti. The organic design built of cast concrete will fascinate both students of architecture and those with only a passing interest in the discipline. Arcosanti has been built primarily with the help of students and volunteers who live here for various lengths of time. To help finance the construction, Soleri designs and sells wind chimes cast in bronze or made of ceramic. These distinctive bells are available at the gift shop.

If you'd like to stay overnight, there are basic accommodations ($25–$75 double) available by reservation. You'll also find a bakery and cafe on the premises. Arcosanti is open daily from 9am to 5pm, and tours are held hourly between 10am and 4pm ($8 suggested donation).

In early 2000, some 71,000 acres of land east of I-17 between Black Canyon City and Cordes Junction were designated the **Agua Fria National Monument,** which is administered by the Bureau of Land Management, Phoenix Field Office, 21605 N. Seventh Ave., Phoenix (© **623/580-5500**). The monument was created to protect the region's numerous prehistoric Native American ruin sites, which date from between A.D. 1250 and 1450 (at least 450 prehistoric sites are known to exist in this area). There is very limited access to the monument, and there are no facilities for visitors. If you'd like to assist with the mapping and recording of archaeological sites here, contact **Archaeological Adventures** (© **623/465-1981;** www. ArchaeologicAdventures.com), which charges $200 per person for a day of documenting unexplored prehistoric sites in the area.

Index

See also Accommodations and Restaurant indexes below.

FROMMER'S® COMPLETE TRAVEL GUIDES

FROMMER'S® DOLLAR-A-DAY GUIDES

FROMMER'S® PORTABLE GUIDES

FROMMER'S® NATIONAL PARK GUIDES

Booked seat 6A, open return.

Rented red 4-wheel drive.

Reserved cabin, no running water.

Discovered space.

With over 700 airlines, 50,000 hotels, 50 rental car companies and 5,000 cruise and vacation packages, you can create the perfect get-away for you. Choose the car, the room, even the ground you walk on.

Travelocity.com
A Sabre Company
Go Virtually Anywhere.